| Date Due | | | |
|---|---|---|---|
| | | | |
| | | | |
| | | | |
| | | | |
| | | | |
| | | | |
| | | | |
| | | | |
| | | | |
| | | | |
| | | | |
| | | | |
| | | | |
| | | | |
| | | | |
| | | | |
| | | | |

# The Trial of Jean-Baptiste M.



Robert Gurik

translated by Allan Van Meer

published with assistance from the Canada Council

**Talonbooks**
**201 1019 East Cordova**
**Vancouver**
**British Columbia V6A 1M8**
**Canada**

This book was typeset and designed by Beverly Matsu, and printed by Gordon Fidler in September, 1974.

First printing: September 1974

Talonplays are edited by Peter Hay.



First published as *Le Proces de Jean-Baptiste M.* by Les Editions Lemeac Inc., Montreal, P.Q. Published by arrangement with Les Editions Lemeac Inc.

ISBN 0-88922-057-3

# Introduction

One of the commonest commonplaces of Canadian culture is to remark about the absence of cross-fertilization between its two official languages. In a country where senior civil servants are legally tortured in government-sponsored language laboratories as a prerequisite for promotion, the equally government-sponsored CBC/Radio-Canada provoked almost a sensation (and bags full of wrathful mail from the chauvinist fringe in both camps) with a harmless 90 minute bilingual entertainment around the first drawing of the Olympic Lottery.

Art, we are sometimes told, transcends politics. So we might have expected literature to flow thicker and faster than bilingual notices at federal airports. Yet, there is only one thing rarer than a French Canadian play produced by an English Canadian theatre, and that's *vice versa.* The exceptions, works by Gratien Gelinas or lately of Michel Tremblay, confirm the rule. The Vancouver Playhouse, along with most of the other regional theatres, has never produced a Quebecois play, even in the Sixties, when it was a hotbed for new works by West Coast playwrights. Tremblay's plays are isolated productions in one or two major cities; the St. Lawrence Centre's version of *Les Belles Soeurs* was not followed by a coast-to-coast epidemic of the play, as with every Neil Simon Broadway hit of two seasons back, or even David French's *Leaving Home.*

Why?

Well, some claim it is a problem of translation. It seems strange in a bilingual country, which supports hordes of official translators. The difficulties evaporate when it comes to a script from France, or when the Theatre du Nouveau Monde needs an American or British play. Shakespeare has been played in most of the civilized tongues of the world and he is not that easy to comprehend in English.

It is not so much a language problem, the argument continues, as a cultural one. A Quebecois play translated, especially from *joual,* has a secret language of topical jokes and political references, which simply does not penetrate the English-Canadian consciousness. How true that is — of Aristophanes, O'Casey and any number of foreign, dead authors. On the other hand, the rationale advanced currently by Quebecois intellectuals, that Canada is just another foreign country to them, may explain their state of mind but certainly does not answer the question. Quite the contrary, Canada — Quebec included — loves foreign plays much more than her own. One of the most effective ways of assuring more productions for them would be to perpetrate the disguise that they are foreign works.

In any case, when it comes down to certain writers or a particular play, the generalizations are even less excusable. Robert Gurik is a French Canadian playwright, living and well-known in Quebec, whose works are as transcendent of place and time as any play that I have read or seen. The only exception would be his early satire, *Hamlet, Prince de Quebec,* which, as the title reveals, is a Quebecois equivalent of *Macbird,* many of whose characters who replace those of Shakespeare have now faded from the Canadian political scene.

But all of his subsequent major works, like *Le Pendu* (*The Hanged Man*) which swept the prizes at the Dominion Drama Festival in Centennial year; or *API 2967*, a utopian satire produced in the same year; or indeed the present work — these are all universally intelligible parables for the contemporary stage, and none the less Quebecois for that. The reverse is true: art that is rooted in time and place, and confidently so, often stands a greater chance of overcoming cultural barriers than works that are trying self-consciously to be international and universally appealing.

Jean-Baptiste M. is an ordinary man caught in the Kafkaesque vise of our multi-national corporate society. If he has a surname, it does not matter; Jean-Baptiste is a completely unimportant hero. The first English language production of the play at the Globe Theatre in Regina underlined this fact by calling the play *The Trial of Mr. What's His Name.* On the other hand, the corporation that he worked for, Dutron, would be called that in any one of the countless countries where it has branch offices. The names of its products are all synthetic words, untranslatable and wholly transferable. The story too is basically nothing more than a newspaper item: 'Fired Employee Shoots Bosses.' What Gurik explores is the individual case-history behind the headline and gives dramatic coherence to what appears to be a senseless act, though less deliberate than Camus' *l'acte gratuite.* Jean-Baptiste's life story as it unravels before a chorus that changes from victims into jurors and judges, is rich in its very ordinariness: it is a life as pointless as its final act of rebellion. Gurik injects and sustains one theme throughout which bathes the play in irony: Jean-Baptiste never for one moment questions the futility of his own existence or the usefulness of the Dutron Corporation. All he wants is to make his mark in Dutron, and he works extra hard to prove his worth to his superiors. When he goes to see his bosses on the final morning, it is with the intention of persuading them to rehire him, to convince them of his ability.

The Quebecois aspect of the play is palpable and not in the least mysterious. Jean-Baptiste M. is born in Ottawa of a French father and an English mother. In the original French text, after his birth, some of the jurors gush over the baby in English: 'A lovely baby!' or 'He is going to be a real Canadian'; a little later: 'A true Canadian', and his name is called 'a true Canadian name'. Jean-Baptiste constantly pushes his knowledge of English as a plus when he tries to get a job. Yet, all his life, J-B. has had only menial jobs, despite his ambition to fit into the system, his eagerness to devote himself completely to work, despite his linguistic abilities in a bilingual country. Jean-Baptiste M., who thinks he could be Prime Minister, is doomed to complete failure, not because of his prison record, but simply because he is born a French Canadian. The play's dramatic impact is the more intense by the fact that this is never made explicitly. Instead, it is constantly demonstrated.

It is fitting for a play with such a theme to receive its first English production not at the National Art Centre or any other sanctum of official bilingual culture, nor at the heavily subsidized bastions of our Anglo-American heritage: the major regional theatres. Of the more established companies, the Globe at Regina retains more than any other a pioneer spirit of struggle, with inadequate premises or finances but growing audiences. Recently I watched the artistic directors, Ken and Sue Kramer, who constitute over one-third of the administrative staff, sweep up after their show until midnight. I pinched myself. I felt in a time warp, taken back into the remote history of Canadian theatre, all the way back – to six or seven years ago.

Peter Hay<br>Fort Langley, B.C.<br>June, 1974

*Le Proces de Jean-Baptiste M.* was first performed at the Theatre du Nouveau Monde in Montreal, P.Q., on October 12, 1972, with the following company:

Jean-Pierre Bergeron
Dorothy Berryman
Emmanuel Charpentier
Jean-Pierre Chartrand
Sophie Clement
Huguette Gervais
Marc Gregoire
Jacques Lavallee
Gilbert Lepage
Jean-Louis Millette
Rejean Roy
Yvan Saintonge

Directed by Roland LaRoche
Sets and Costumes by Renee Noiseux
Assisted by Pierre Labonte
Lighting by Michel Beaulieu
Music by Emmanuel Charpentier

*The Trial of Jean-Baptiste M.* was also performed under the title, *The Trial of Mr. What's His Name,* at the Globe Theatre in Regina, Saskatchewan, on February 26, 1974, with the following company:

Mario Crudo
Kyra Harper
David McCulley
David Miller
Judith Orban
Naomi St. John
Robert Sime
Leslie Stolzenberger, Jr.
Jim Timmins

Directed by Roland LaRoche
Stage Managed by Phyllis Cowie
Wardrobe by Marian Buller

# Act One

*Music made of a montage of the noises of typewriters, telephones, cars, telexes, industrial machines, whistles, time-clocks, footsteps, running, coughing, sneezing, cafeteria dishes, etc.*

*A pause, and then a deafening explosion coinciding with a spotlight on the face of a man with a ghastly wound in the head.*

*A pause, then a second explosion coinciding with a second spot on the face of another fatally wounded man.*

*Pause, followed by a third explosion, and a third character appears with a bleeding hole in his chest. The victims reel off their identities.*

**MARSHALL, lst victim:**

Roy Marshall
Married to Jennifer Rowland
Father of two children

**MARSHALL, 1st victim:**

Industrial Sales Inspector, fifteen years
in the service of the Dutron Corporation.

**McPHERSON, 2nd victim:**

Doug McPherson
Ex-fighter pilot with the R.C.A.F.
Married to Kate Rooney
Father of three children
Sales Director, fourteen years
in the service of the Dutron Corporation.

**LALONDE, 3rd victim:**

Dave Lalonde
Born in Ottawa, Ontario
Married to Marion Leslie
Father of two children
Sales Director for Eastern Canada, nine years
In the service of the Dutron Corporation.

*Spot downstage where JEAN-BAPTISTE M. is dialing a telephone number.*

**JEAN-BAPTISTE:**

May I speak to Christiane M., please. *waits* Hello, Christiane . . . Jean-Baptiste. *pause* I just called to tell you, it's done. *pause* Got my job back? . . . No! I shot my bosses. I love you. *He hangs up, then very calmly dials another number.* Hello, Dutron? . . . I'd like to speak to the officer in charge . . . *long pause* Hello . . . yes . . . I'm the one that killed them.

*Blackout. When the lights come back up the scene is the courtroom. M. enters in handcuffs. The JUDGES are the three victims and traces of their fatal wounds are noticeable.*

*Percussion.*

**CRIER:**

The Crown versus Jean-Baptiste M.
For the crime of murder
Upon three counts
For the bereavement
Of three families
Of their means of support
For the willful injury
Of a great enterprise
For contempt
Of the accepted order
On this day of grace
Nineteen hundred and seventy-two.
Gentlemen, the Court is in session!

*The trial opens.*

*Percussion.*

**JUDGES:**

Let each man be free
To speak what he knows
To speak what he thinks
To do what he must
That justice may triumph.

*Percussion.*

**CRIER:**

Jean-Baptiste M., born in Ottawa.

**FATHER:**

Son of Victor M., army officer, retired.

**MOTHER:**

And of Jenny, housewife.

**JEAN-BAPTISTE:**

Three sisters: Louisette, aged 36.

**MOTHER:**

Employed by Avon.

**FATHER:**
Cosmetics.

**JEAN-BAPTISTE:**
Sophie, aged 34.

**MOTHER:**
Employed by the Federal Government.

**FATHER:**
Politics.

**JEAN-BAPTISTE:**
Helene, aged 32.

**MOTHER:**
Employed by the Dominion Bank.

**FATHER:**
Economics.

**JEAN-BAPTISTE:**
Two brothers: Jean, aged 33.

**MOTHER:**
Member of the Canadian Air Force.

**FATHER:**
Aviation.

**JEAN-BAPTISTE:**
Louis, aged 25.

**MOTHER:**
Instructor in physical culture at the Health Spa salon.

**FATHER:**
Recreation.

*Percussion.*

**JEAN-BAPTISTE:**

I was born on the 7th of October, 1943, in Ottawa.

**LALONDE, judge:**

Did he suffer any deformities at birth which might constitue extenuating circumstances in this trial? Was he cross-eyed?

**McPHERSON, judge:**

Did he have flat feet?
Was he mongoloid?
Was he mute?
Blind?
Did he show good reflexes?

**MARSHALL, judge:**

Had his mother used any drugs before his birth?
Was his father alcoholic?
Did he enter society via Caesarian section?

**LALONDE, judge:**

Were there any indications of post-operative shock?
Was he a wanted child, or the result of an accident?
Was he baptised?

**MOTHER:**

He was in perfect health. He was the kind of baby every family dreams of.

*Percussion.*

**CRIER:**

The witnesses will come forward.

**JUDGES:**

Let the witnesses confirm
Their ability to state
That according to their recollections
Jean-Baptiste was born
Sound of body and of mind
And that he was received
Into a nourishing environment.

*The JUROR-WITNESSES surround the "baby" JEAN-BAPTISTE M. MARSHALL has left the judges' bench to become the FATHER. The MOTHER is at his side.*

**1st JUROR:** *proud*
A handsome specimen; nine pounds, a fine figure of a man.

**2nd JUROR:**
I thought he'd never make it out; it felt like he was hanging on in there for dear life, just didn't want to poke his nose outside.

**3rd JUROR:** *feeling M.*
He's well built; look at these arms.

**4th JUROR:** *spreading open M.'s eyes*
Beautiful blue eyes!

**5th JUROR:** *opening M.'s mouth*
He doesn't have any teeth.

**6th JUROR:**
You didn't have any either at that age.

**5th JUROR:**
Ah! –

**7th JUROR:**
A lovely baby!

**8th JUROR:**
He's going to be a real Canadian.

**LALONDE, judge:** *banging the gavel*
Just like his father!

*JEAN-BAPTISTE is passed around like a sheet of paper. At the end of the circle he is dropped to one side.*

*The following lines are spoken during this action.*

**8th JUROR:**
Big strong boy like that, he'll be a fireman.

**7th JUROR:**
Or a policeman.

**6th JUROR:**
Or an M.P.

**5th JUROR:**
M.P. – not a bad idea.

**4th JUROR:** *putting his hand on M.'s genitals*
At any rate, he's a man.

**3rd JUROR:**
He looks bright, he'll be a teacher.

**2nd JUROR:**
He's well built . . . a career in the army for him.

**lst JUROR:**
A true Canadian.

**McPHERSON, judge:** *banging the gavel*
Like me . . . and his father.

*The passing in the circle finishes.*

**MOTHER:**
The important thing is that he's in good health. We'll name him Jean-Baptiste.

**9th JUROR:**
What's his name?

**4th JUROR:**
They gonna call him J.B.!

**9th JUROR:**
A genuine Canadian name.

**LALONDE, judge:** *banging the gavel*
Like mine. I was born in Ottawa, and my name is Dave . . . Dave Lalonde.

**JUROR-WITNESSES:** *call JEAN-BAPTISTE like a puppy*
J.B. . . . , here J.B. . . . come on boy . . . that's a fella . . . here J.B. . . . *etc. rising to a shouting crescendo*

*JEAN-BAPTISTE M. starts to scream, picks up the rifle, and shoots.*

*Blackout, and the lights of the first scene come up, i.e., the three spots on the three victims, in their original positions. The spots go out, and the general lighting comes up.*

*Percussion.*

**CRIER:**
June, 1959.

**JEAN-BAPTISTE:**
I complete my elementary schooling in Ottawa.

*A JUROR-WITNESS leaves his bench and becomes the 1st EMPLOYER. Other characters follow suit through the rest of this scene.*

**CRIER:**
January, 1960.

**JEAN-BAPTISTE:**
I am 17 years old.

**1st EMPLOYER:**
Best clothing.

**JEAN-BAPTISTE:**
I'm hired as a sweeper.

**CRIER:**
April 8, 1960.

**JEAN-BAPTISTE:**
I quit for a better job.

**CRIER:**
April 15, 1960.

**2nd EMPLOYER:**
Canadian Pacific Railways.

**JEAN-BAPTISTE:**
Office boy. I leave after a month for a job closer to home.

**CRIER:**
May, 1960.

**3rd EMPLOYER:**
Dominion Stores.

**JEAN-BAPTISTE:**
Packer.

**CRIER:**
August, 1960.

**JEAN-BAPTISTE:**
I join the Canadian Army.

**McPHERSON, judge:**
Like me and his father.

*Percussion – military drums.*

*The JUROR-WITNESSES come down to be soldiers. They surround M. and congratulate him.*

**JEAN-BAPTISTE:**
I never laughed so hard in my life.

**1st SOLDIER:**
When you shaved his head . . .

**2nd SOLDIER:**
The guy didn't dare say a word.

**3rd SOLDIER:**
Till he got a look at himself in the mirror afterwards.

**JEAN-BAPTISTE:**
He let out a squeal like a stuck pig!

**1st SOLDIER:**
One of the best initiations we ever had!

*McPHERSON arrives, he is the commander.*

**McPHERSON:**
Attention! Private J.B.M.!

*M. steps out of the ranks, stands at attention. McPHERSON barks his orders* faster, harder, run, stop; to the ground: one-two, one-two . . . *etc.*

*JEAN-BAPTISTE M. performs the exercises alone while his buddies, at first silent, gradually begin laughing, working up to a huge, monstrous, general laugh.*

*McPHERSON finally stops the exercises and JEAN-BAPTISTE M., exhausted, falls back into line, only to be called up again.*

Private J.B.M.

*JEAN-BAPTISTE steps out of the ranks.*

This was to give you some pleasant memories before your departure. *He takes out a document which is M.'s dishonourable discharge orders for having given a recruit a haircut during initiation. He reads:*

For disobeying in his line of duty; orders; for showing no respect for laws; or the discipline of the army of our gracious Queen, we declare in her name that Jean-Bap-

**McPHERSON:**

tiste M. is ejected from the ranks. This judgement is effective from this very date: November 12th, 1961.

*The end of the reading is punctuated by a drum roll which disperses the "army game".*

*McPHERSON returns to his judge's place and MARSHALL comes down to take the part of the FATHER.*

**CRIER:**

November, 1961.

**JEAN-BAPTISTE:**

I'm kicked out of the army, I go back to my family.

*JEAN-BAPTISTE M. returns, rifle in hand. His family and friends of the family await him.*

**MOTHER:** *in a lunge towards her son, checked by the FATHER*

Jean-Baptiste!

**FATHER:** *advancing towards his son*

Kicked out of the army! Shaving a soldier's head, how'd you like to have somebody do that to you, make you a laughing stock and have everybody avoid you like the plague? Where are your brains, anyway? ! All you think about is playing the fool; well, life isn't just fun and games, boy, life is tough and it hurts. Do you think it was a pleasure for your mother and I all these years scrimping and saving just so you could make something of yourself? We all work long and hard every day earning ourselves some security from everything that threatens us out there.

*The FATHER, losing control, unleashes the bitter aggressiveness of the protagonists by slapping M. several times until he falls on his knees. The FATHER seizes his rifle from him, which is passed from hand to hand. Strident yell from JEAN-BAPTISTE M.*

**FATHER:**

Thought you were big enough for my boots already, eh? You may be grown up, but you still haven't got what it takes. You're not a man yet.

*JEAN-BAPTISTE M. has recoiled from his FATHER. The protagonists are now wild, hysterical in their gestures, but their tone and voice remain normal. He tries to retrieve his rifle, but without success.*

**1st WOMAN:** *pulling him by the hair towards her*

You think it's a joke spending eight hours in front of a typewriter and coming home to wash the kids' filthy faces? !

**1st MAN:** *hitting him*

While this big shot's clowning around, I get up at six-thirty in the morning to get to work and don't get home before six at night.

**2nd WOMAN:** *catching him and shoving his head in her skirts*

You have to earn your security and your freedom, you have to learn to go without a lot of things, a lot of satisfactions.

**2nd MAN:** *grabbing his genitals*

It's tough being a man, it's not enough just being born. To produce, you have to make sacrifices.

*JEAN-BAPTISTE M. screams, extricates himself, retrieves his rifle and shoots at the three JUDGES.*

*Blackout. The three spots come up again on the three victims – dark, then general lighting.*

*The JUROR-WITNESSES have taken their seats again. Only JEAN-BAPTISTE M. is left in the centre, and, off to the side, his FATHER and MOTHER.*

**JEAN-BAPTISTE:**

Alright, so this is good-bye, but just let me tell you before I go, I'll make good, just as good as you. I'll be wearing your boots yet. And I'm going to have a wife myself too, and kids, and a house, and furniture and a car. You want me to become a man? Well, I'll damn well be one! I've got everything it takes to be happy; I'm healthy, I'm smart enough, I know how to read, write, count, speak good English, I've got guts, I like people, I'm honest. And I'm going to be somebody, this is a free country, everybody's got a fair chance, anybody can become Prime Minister . . . O.K.?

*Percussion.*

*JEAN-BAPTISTE resumes his original place.*

*The JUDGES take their places.*

**CRIER:**

Gentlemen, the Court is in session!

*Percussion.*

The Crown versus Jean–Baptiste M.
For the crime of murder
Upon three counts
For the bereavement
Of three families
Of their means of support
For the willful injury
Of a great enterprise
For disruption
Of the accepted order
On this day of grace
Nineteen hundred and seventy-two.
The trial will continue.

JUDGES:

Let each man be free
To speak what he knows
To speak what he thinks
To do what he must
That justice may triumph.

*Percussion.*

The Dutron World Products Corporation
The injured party
Victim of the criminal act
The company that produces
For society:

Kantron nylons
Porlon acrylics
Kraly textiles
Bypar carpeting
Teflon fibre
Coron rope
Lacron polyesters
Refrigerants, aerosols
Solvents, peroxides
Paints and enamels
Dynamite and other explosives
Frayon
Delux
Lactates
Teflons
Dulete
Liners
Films, tubes, resins,
Vinyls, acids, dyes,
Insecticides
Cellophanes
Celluloids
Porfal
Dutex
Fibrex
Valar
Cor-flex

**JUDGES:**

Bortel
Mylon
Teflar
Klytar
Katon
Mitron
Bucinth
Debrin
Salyn
Diprene
And what have you.
The greatest chemical empire
In the world
Thousands of employees
Dozens of factories
Millions of capital shares:
The Dutron Corporation
Injured party
Innocent victim
versus Jean-Baptiste M.

*Percussion.*

**JEAN-BAPTISTE:**

I look for a job.

**CRIER:**

Let all those who can testify
As to his actions
Come into this circle

**JUDGES:**

And let each man be free
To speak what he knows
To speak what he thinks
To do what he must
That justice may triumph.

*Percussion.*

**CRIER:**
August 13, 1962.

**JEAN-BAPTISTE:**
I present myself at the Unemployment Insurance Office.

*McPHERSON, civil servant, consults his files.*

*All the witnesses come down to make a waiting line. They chatter among themselves and suddenly hush themselves when McPHERSON speaks.*

**McPHERSON:**
Monsieur M., you have a job; you have been hired by Steinberg's Supermarkets.

*All the JUROR-WITNESSES become JEAN-BAPTISTE M.'s and go up to thank McPHERSON.*

**THE JEAN-BAPTISTE M.'s:**
Thank you . . . thank you . . . thank you ever so much *etc.* . . . When do I start? . . . When . . . do I start . . . *etc.*

**McPHERSON:** *to each one*
Tomorrow.

**The JEAN-BAPTISTE M.'s:**
Tomorrow?

**JUDGES:**
Yes, tomorrow!

**CRIER:**
August 14, 1962!

**JEAN-BAPTISTE:**
I am hired as Service Manager.

*The last JEAN-BAPTISTE M. takes McPHERSON's place and becomes the manager of Steinberg's. The employees come in to work at Steinberg's. JEAN-BAPTISTE M. stands apart, behind.*

MANAGER: *to the first employee who arrives*
Two minutes late. That'll be a half-hour docked from your next cheque.

1st EMPLOYEE:
But . . . the snow storm . . .

MANAGER:
In the middle of August!

1st EMPLOYEE:
I mean . . .

MANAGER:
Not interested!

*Each EMPLOYEE, after having passed before the MANAGER, becomes a boss himself, forming a veritable wall by the time JEAN-BAPTISTE comes to intervene.*

2nd MANAGER: *to 2nd EMPLOYEE*
There's carts sitting around in all the aisles. This place looks more like a dump than a supermarket.

2nd EMPLOYEE:
But . . .

2nd MANAGER:
Don't give me any buts . . . I don't want excuses; I want results – clear aisles that people can move around in.

2nd EMPLOYEE:
But . . .

**2nd MANAGER:**

Are you dense or what? Carts, that's plain English, isn't it?! If it isn't done in ten minutes, you're fired!

*2nd EMPLOYEE becomes boss.*

**3rd MANAGER:**

I noticed you having another private conference with the girl at checkout number three.

**3rd EMPLOYEE:**

Well, you were young once, yourself!

**3rd MANAGER:**

Company time isn't the time for that. While you're yakking away, the Cordon Bleu meat ball cans are getting mixed up with the Dr. Ballard's.

*The 3rd EMPLOYEE becomes boss.*

**4th MANAGER:**

Understood?

**4th EMPLOYEE:**

The customer is always king.

**4th MANAGER:**

If there were no customers, there'd be no Steinberg's; it doesn't take a university degree to grasp that! So get to work!

*The 4th EMPLOYEE becomes boss. JEAN-BAPTISTE comes in and plants himself in front of the bosses.*

**JEAN-BAPTISTE:**

It's no good, it can't go on like this. I can't stand it any more.

**5th MANAGER:**

Can't stand what?

JEAN-BAPTISTE:

The way you treat the little guys like dogs. You take advanatage of their position to keep them down. The little guy's a person like you and me.

5th MANAGER:

You'd rather I let them come in anytime they felt like, and turned the store into a social club?

JEAN-BAPTISTE:

That's not what I said.

5th MANAGER:

Listen, J.B., you were made Service Manager because you're bright, alert, and you can think for yourself, but don't get it into your head that you're somebody you're not.

JEAN-BAPTISTE:

Just because I've got a good job, I'm not going to put up with the employees being treated like shit. I want to see the president.

5th MANAGER:

The president of what?

JEAN-BAPTISTE:

The president of the company.

1st MANAGER:

Tell me, J.B., just what's your problem? What are you after?

2nd MANAGER:

The big bad guy who's responsible for everything? Who forces the poor weaklings to work?

3rd MANAGER:

I've got news for you, J.B. There's no big bad guy. He doesn't exist, you understand?

4th MANAGER:
This store has to meet a sales quota and show a profit; otherwise it won't exist and there'd be no employees.

1st MANAGER:
My duty is to see that those objectives are met, and that means that the employees have got to respect the rules and regulations of the company. And it wasn't me who made up those rules, they were communicated to me by my boss, the District Manager.

JEAN-BAPTISTE:
I want to see the District Manager.

5th MANAGER:
But he's not the big bad guy. He didn't make up the rules!

2nd MANAGER:
He received them from the Marketing Director.

3rd MANAGER:
And don't tell me you want to see the Marketing Director.

4th MANAGER:
Because he received them from the General Manager.

1st MANAGER:
Who received his orders from the Board of Directors who applied the recommendations of the report they commissioned from a firm of management consultants.

5th MANAGER:
Do you think you know more than somebody with a degree in management counselling, young man?

JEAN-BAPTISTE:
You're not going to get results by putting down the little guy.

**5th MANAGER:** *sarcastic*

Maybe you should be on the Board of Directors, eh?

**2nd MANAGER:**

And don't think you'll find the big bad guy there either, because the Board executive follows only the wishes of the shareholders . . .

**3rd MANAGER:**

Who demand, and rightly so, a certain return on their investment . . .

**4th MANAGER:**

. . . And the shareholder is the man-in-the-street, the customer; he's you and me . . .

**EVERYBODY:**

. . . And the guy next door!

**JEAN-BAPTISTE:**

Knock it off with these scare stories! To hear you talk, I ought to end up believing it's me that's shafting the employees, and that Mr. Steinberg doesn't exist.

**1st MANAGER:**

You just won't understand, will you?

**2nd MANAGER:**

You think you're so much nicer than the next guy?

**3rd MANAGER:**

There's a whole gang of guys busting their asses to get a job like you've got.

**4th MANAGER:**

But Mr. Jean-Baptiste M. isn't satisfied, that's not enough for him, he has to play the martyr as well!

**5th MANAGER:**

You want to get to know Mr. Steinberg?

3rd MANAGER:
Well, I'm going to help you out; you can pay a little visit to Mr. Steinberg's treasurer.

2nd MANAGER:
That's already a step in the right direction . . .

3rd MANAGER:
And you can ask him for your paycheck, mentioning, by the way, that it's your last one.

4th MANAGER:
O.K.?

5th MANAGER:
And I don't want to see you in here again, except . . . as a customer.

*Percussion.*

CRIER:
April 2, 1963.

5th EMPLOYER:
Banque de Montreal – Bank of Montreal.

JEAN-BAPTISTE:
Bank clerk for one week. I'm let go because my father won't endorse me.

CRIER:
April 23, 1963.

6th EMPLOYER:
Sixth Employer, Canadien National – Canadian National Railways.

JEAN-BAPTISTE:
File clerk.

CRIER:
May, 1965.

**JEAN-BAPTISTE:**
I lose my job for a stupid thing that costs me five months in jail.

**EVERYBODY:**
Jail!

*They retreat, and assemble into a jury again.*

**LALONDE, judge:**
You are accused of attempted burglary of a private home. Jean Baptiste M., what have you to answer in your defense?

**JEAN-BAPTISTE:**
Your Honour, I got dragged into that B & E. I didn't know my friend was planning it, and when it happened I was just . . . like . . . scared shitless.

**LALONDE, judge:**
You mean "frozen in your tracks"?

**JEAN-BAPTISTE:**
That's right, your Honour.

**LALONDE, judge:**
I see here also, that this is not your first offense . . . Brampton, Ontario, does that mean anything to you?

**EVERYBODY:** *murmurs of surprise and indignation*
Mm-hmm . . . oh! . . . well, well . . . mm . . . well then . . . .

**LALONDE, judge:**
Order! Silence, or else I'll adjourn this court. *Order is restored.*

**JEAN-BAPTISTE:**
Yes, it does, your Honour.

**LALONDE, judge:**
Nature of the offence?

**JEAN-BAPTISTE:**
It's written in your file, your Honour.

**LALONDE, judge:**
I would like to hear you say it.

**JEAN-BAPTISTE:**
It's embarrassing.

**LALONDE, judge:**
I'm waiting.

**JEAN-BAPTISTE:**
I was going for a walk . . . a guy comes up to me.

*A man leaves the jury.*

*JEAN-BAPTISTE addresses the jury while the man relives the scene in Brampton, off to one side.*

**MAN:**
Hey! Think you could do me a favour?

**JEAN-BAPTISTE:** *explaining*
I didn't say no. I'm an obliging sort by nature.

**MAN:**
My fly's open; could you just do it up for me?

**JEAN-BAPTISTE:**
Your Honour, I said to him straight, right there: Do it up yourself, you've got two hands!

**MAN:**
My hands are kinda greasy; I don't want to get my pants dirty, I just bought them.

**JEAN-BAPTISTE:**
It seemed to me, your Honour, that he should have been able to manage by himself. Which is what he did anyway.

*The MAN closes his zipper.*

Then he offered me a cigarette and I took it. *M. takes a cigarette, puts it in his mouth. At this point the JURORS begin caressing and groping each other – mixed couples, then couples of the same sex. Meanwhile the two JUDGES are stroking each others' hands.*

MAN:
Hey! I like the way you put that in your mouth.

JEAN-BAPTISTE:
Well, where else would you expect me to put it, your Honour?

MAN: *laughing*
You're funny, you are, Christ, are you funny!

*JEAN-BAPTISTE moves on. The MAN, a little abashed, continues his approach.* What do you do anyway?

JEAN-BAPTISTE:
I'm looking for a job.

MAN:
Yeah? Well, if I were as good-looking as you, I'd be a millionaire by now. You get what I mean?

JEAN-BAPTISTE:
Of course I got what he meant, your Honour. I mean, I wasn't born yesterday, but I'm not one of those types.

MAN:
Anyway, if I was a boss I'd hire you and you could stay in bed all day if you wanted to. Know what I mean?

JEAN-BAPTISTE: *more and more annoyed*
I didn't feel like playing games anymore. I didn't answer him.

**MAN:**

Come on, don't tell me you've never slept with a man? It's great, just wait till you try it, you don't need any experience anyway, I'll teach you. *His hand reaches down to his fly. The scene in the jury-box is in paroxysm.* Come over here with me right now, you're giving me an awful hard-on.

*The Jury stops short at J.B.'s outburst of anger.*

**JEAN-BAPTISTE:** *furious*

You fucking pansy! It's nuts like you that're fucking up the whole world! You make me sick, you make me puke, you're not a man, you're worse than a fuckin' animal!

**MAN:** *cutting him off*

Stop it! Be quiet! . . . O.K., I'm taking off . . . just calm down . . . I'll leave you alone . . .

**JEAN-BAPTISTE:**

You oughta be locked up, all of you – pigs! Filth! Try to drag everything into your muck, you can't live like human beings!

**MAN:**

You ought to show this guy that it's an offence to assault people!

*Two people from the jury come down to restrain him and allow the MAN, who is still in Brampton anyway, as at the start, to make an awkward getaway.*

**LALONDE, judge:**

So this is your second offense . . .

**JEAN-BAPTISTE:**

But your Honour, that was a homosexual! It's terrible what a person like that could do, rot our kids' minds for the rest of their lives; they can rot a whole society even. Something's got to be done about it. And the

**JEAN-BAPTISTE:**
government's not going to do anything. They're not men even.

**LALONDE, judge:**
What do you consider to be a man, Jean-Baptiste M.? Who breaks into a private home and assaults a man, or the one that accosted you in Brampton, Ontario?

**JEAN-BAPTISTE:** *makes his grand declaration to the accompaniment of a crescendo of percussion*

A man is one who respects the law and who works with his whole mind to advance his fellows and himself.

**CRIER:**
May 15, 1965.

**LALONDE, judge:**
The Court sentences Jean-Baptiste M. to six months in . . .

**EVERYBODY:**
Jail!

*Percussion.*

*Two JUROR-WITNESSES come down to be PRISONERS who welcome M. They circle round him.*

**1st PRISONER:**
Hey! A new customer.

**2nd PRISONER:**
How long you in for?

**JEAN-BAPTISTE:**
Six months.

**1st PRISONER:**
Shoplifting?

**JEAN-BAPTISTE:**
No, B & E.

**2nd PRISONER:**
First time?

**JEAN-BAPTISTE:** *hesitating*
Yes.

**1st PRISONER:**
Thought so.

*The two PRISONERS laugh. They shove him around more and more, paw him over as in the childhood scene.*

You're a clean cut little bastard, ain't you?

**2nd PRISONER:**
A real fashion plate.

**1st PRISONER:**
You know what he reminds me of?

**2nd PRISONER:**
What?

**1st PRISONER:**
The guys that do the deodorant ads.

**2nd PRISONER:**
Yeah! You're right! And the economy car ads!

**1st PRISONER:**
And the electric home-comfort heating, those are fuckin' ridiculous!

**2nd PRISONER:**
I got it! I got it!

**1st PRISONER:**
What?

**2nd PRISONER:**
The guy that can buy anything and trips around the world on his American Express credit card, like on TV.

**1st PRISONER:**
That's him! It's gotta be him!

**2nd PRISONER:**
Uh-uh, couldn't be him, if it was him he'd just get up and flash his card and split (click-click) like that. Wouldn't he?

**1st PRISONER:**
If it ain't him maybe it's his brother.

**2nd PRISONER:** *leering*
Or his sister?

**JEAN-BAPTISTE:** *pushed too far, shouts*
Lay off, wouldya! Just lay off!

*The two others retreat and change their tone.*

**1st PRISONER:**
O.K., you don't have to get uptight, you gotta fool around once in awhile.

**JEAN-BAPTISTE:**
I want out.

**2nd PRISONER:**
Just stay cool, you've got six whole months, save your strength.

**1st PRISONER:**
You'll find out, it isn't all bad. Prison's about the only place where you can be whatever you want, nobody's gonna stop you. The only things missin' are the little extras.

**2nd PRISONER:**

But you've got time to work on that, you've got all the time in the world. There's no rat race in here, you can take it easy.

*They talk very slowly.*

**1st PRISONER:**

I think you really are the guy with the credit card.

**2nd PRISONER:**

And if you're not, you've got plenty of time to work on it. You've got six months.

**1st PRISONER:**

One hundred and eighty-three days.

**2nd PRISONER:**

Four thousand, three hundred and ninety-eight hours.

**JEAN-BAPTISTE:**

I wouldn't mind that, being the guy with the American Express card. I could go into the classiest restaurants and get myself a big new car just showing my card. I could get married, splurge a bit on a house, oh, not a mansion or anything, no, just a small place, nice and clean, with electric heating. Then we could take holidays, see the ocean . . . I've never seen it . . . in Florida! And then I'd have a job, a real one! A job for life, where I'd be doing something useful, where I'd be respected, a job with secretaries, and telephones, and an elevator . . . a real job!

*Percussion.*

**CRIER:**

September, 1965.

**JEAN-BAPTISTE:**

Owing to my good behaviour, society releases me after four months' detention.

**EVERYBODY:**
Bravo!

*Percussion.*

*The circle of EMPLOYERS forms again.*

**CRIER:**
October, 1965.

**7th EMPLOYER:**
Fairmont Motors.

**JEAN-BAPTISTE:**
Car jockey.

**CRIER:**
November, 1965.

**JEAN-BAPTISTE:**
I have a fight with the mechanic who treats me like a dog, like garbage, like shit . . .

**CRIER:**
November, 1965.

**8th EMPLOYER:**
Librairie Laffitte – Laffitte Bookstore.

**JEAN-BAPTISTE:**
Sales clerk, for three months. Left unemployed when bookstore burns down.

**CRIER:**
April, 1966.

**9th EMPLOYER:**
Librairie Pinson – Pinson Bookstore.

**JEAN-BAPTISTE:**
Sales clerk for one week. Fired for reasons unknown. From May 66 until June 66 I look for a job again.

**CRIER:**
June 21, 1966, 8 a.m.

**11th EMPLOYER:**
Multinational Bldg. Credit.

**JEAN-BAPTISTE:**
At 11 a.m., I am fired because I have a criminal record.

**CRIER:**
June 23, 1966.

**12th EMPLOYER:**
Star Traffic Services.

**JEAN-BAPTISTE:**
Receipts clerk.

**CRIER:**
June 29, 1966.

**JEAN-BAPTISTE:**
I get married.

*Percussion.*

*Party music, everybody congratulates J.B.M. Wedding atmosphere.*

**McPHERSON, judge:**
But before his marriage, the accused had nevertheless experienced other relations . . .

**MARSHALL, judge:**
In Brampton, Ontario, for example.

*The jury laughs.*

**LALONDE, judge:**
It is important that we know something of his behaviour outside of his work.

**CRIER:**
Let all those who can testify to the activities of Jean-Baptiste M. come into this circle.

**JUDGES:**
Let each man be free
To speak what he knows
To speak what he thinks
To do what he must
That justice may triumph.

*Percussion.*

**CRIER:**
Mlle. Lafontaine.

**CARMEN:**
Carmen Lafontaine, self-employed.

*A woman comes forward and takes a position near JEAN-BAPTISTE M.*

*JEAN-BAPTISTE M. prowls around her, indecisively.*

This ain't the Granby zoo, kid!

**JEAN-BAPTISTE:** *embarrassed*
I wasn't . . . uh . . . I mean . . . are you Carmen?

**CARMEN:**
Yeah.

**JEAN-BAPTISTE:**
I was sent by a friend.

**CARMEN:**
Mm-hmm, I get ya, so?

**JEAN-BAPTISTE:**
Well, it's for . . .

**CARMEN:**
How old are you?

**JEAN-BAPTISTE:**
Sixteen.

**CARMEN:**
Well, you didn't come down here for a chit-chat; you want a few minutes of my time?

**JEAN-BAPTISTE:**
Well . . . uh . . . I guess so, yeah.

**CARMEN:** *snickering*
I don't have to be an Einstein to figure that out.

**JEAN-BAPTISTE:** *encouraged*
I'm just a little shy.

**CARMEN:**
How do you want it?

**JEAN-BAPTISTE:**
Want what?

**CARMEN:**
All dressed, well-done or rare?

**JEAN-BAPTISTE:**
I think I'd . . . I'd rather have it . . . uh, rare, I guess.

**CARMEN:**
It ain't a question of what you'd rather, it's what you can afford. How much ya got?

**JEAN-BAPTISTE:**
I've got five dollars.

**CARMEN:**
That'll be all dressed . . . come back in half an hour . . . I got an appointment with a regular who likes it raw.

JEAN-BAPTISTE: *panicky*
O.K. . . . thank you . . . in half an hour then, Madame, I mean Mademoiselle . . .

CARMEN:
'S okay, kid.

*Percussion.*

CRIER:
Helene McDonald.

*Another woman comes down to join JEAN-BAPTISTE M. who is getting impatient.*

JEAN-BAPTISTE:
Finally! I've been waiting for you to show for half an hour.

HELENE:
I had an argument with Daddy.

JEAN-BAPTISTE:
Hurry up, we're going to be late for the show.

HELENE:
Wait a minute Jean-Baptiste . . . I came to tell you that it's . . . it's over between us.

JEAN-BAPTISTE:
Over?

HELENE:
Yes, Daddy doesn't think we should see each other anymore.

JEAN-BAPTISTE:
Why? . . .

HELENE:

He says that you're not a good match for me. Daddy's done his law degree, and you'd just never be able to provide me everything that he has.

JEAN-BAPTISTE:

Well, I can work on it.

HELENE:

You haven't even finished school . . . and without a diploma these days, you're nowhere.

JEAN-BAPTISTE:

That's your gang all right, Christ, marry off your lawyers' daughters to doctors, and doctors' daughters to bankers and if any outsider tries to get in there, a swift boot in the ass'll teach him to remember his place.

HELENE:

Oh, come on, Jean-Baptiste, you don't have to be so melodramatic! Besides, Daddy says we're much too young, you're not even eighteen yet.

JEAN-BAPTISTE:

"Daddy says, Daddy says", why the hell don't you go marry Daddy then?

HELENE:

Jean-Baptiste! Daddy was absolutely right, you're nothing but slum trash, and you'll never amount to anything! *She goes off.*

*Percussion.*

CRIER:

Christiane Thetrault.

*CHRISTIANE comes down to join JEAN-BAPTISTE M.*

JEAN-BAPTISTE:

Christiane, I couldn't wait to see you.

**CHRISTIANE:**

Me neither, Jean-Baptiste.

**JEAN-BAPTISTE:**

I had so many things I wanted to tell you, and now that you're here, it's like I'm frozen.

**CHRISTIANE:**

What is it you want to tell me, Jean-Baptiste? That it's over between us?

**JEAN-BAPTISTE:**

No, no! Just the opposite, but I'm afraid the same thing might happen as with my jobs. Everytime I say what I think, when I honestly want to help, it doesn't work. It's like people seem to get scared when you tell things the way they are.

**CHRISTIANE:**

You know that I love you.

**JEAN-BAPTISTE:**

I love you too . . . *making up his mind* I don't have much to offer you, an old car I'm still paying off, a lousy job that doesn't bring in anything.

**CHRISTIANE:**

Why are you telling me this?

**JEAN-BAPTISTE:**

Because I wish we could always be together; I'd like us to get married.

**CHRISTIANE:**

I'd like to live with you too. And you know, I could keep on working.

**JEAN-BAPTISTE:**

That's not all . . . there's something else.

**CHRISTIANE:**

Tell me, I can take it . . . You're already married?

**JEAN-BAPTISTE:**

No! *quickly* I've spent some time in prison, six months . . . twice. *even faster* But the first time, they let me out after four months.

**CHRISTIANE:**

So?

**JEAN-BAPTISTE:**

Well, I've got a record, that sort of marks a guy.

**CHRISTIANE:**

I don't see any scars.

**JEAN-BAPTISTE:**

I'd like to give you something better.

**CHRISTIANE:**

But what you've given me is more important, Jean-Baptiste, your way of caring about me, that's what is really precious, and what you want to be . . . don't worry, you'll make it somehow. And even if you don't, we'll be together. What counts is being happy, not rich.

**JEAN-BAPTISTE:**

Everything is so simple with you; I really feel good for the first time. Like things aren't as complicated as I thought . . . I love you.

**CHRISTIANE:**

I love you.

*Percussion.*

*Celebrating . . . JEAN-BAPTISTE and CHRISTIANE are in front of the JUROR-WITNESSES on the steps of the church. Wedding photographs being taken.*

*The JUDGES pick up their original masks.*

**CRIER:**
December, 1966.

**12th EMPLOYER:**
Star Traffic Services.

**JEAN-BAPTISTE:**
I've just got married, I'm making $48 a week, and I'm fired because I have the gall to ask for a raise.

**CRIER:**
January, 1967.

**13th EMPLOYER:**
Duke Office Supplies.

**JEAN-BAPTISTE:**
Sales clerk.

*A SECRETARY comes in.*

**SECRETARY:**
Mr. M?

**JEAN-BAPTISTE:**
Yes.

**SECRETARY:**
I have some bad news, I'm afraid we'll have to dismiss you.

**JEAN-BAPTISTE:**
Have to? But why? Isn't my work satisfactory?

**SECRETARY:**
No, it isn't that, on the contrary . . . You do have a criminal record, don't you?

**JEAN-BAPTISTE:**
Yes . . . but . . .

**SECRETARY:**
Please understand, that doesn't make any difference to us, but . . . here! Ask this gentleman, he will explain it to you.

**JEAN-BAPTISTE:**
Is he the boss?

**SECRETARY:**
No, he's the insurance agent for the company.

*She withdraws.*

**JEAN-BAPTISTE:** *to the man who has come forward*
Sir? . . .

**AGENT:**
Vic Young, for the Ritual.

**JEAN-BAPTISTE:**
It's because of you that I'm being fired, isn't it?

**AGENT:**
Because of me? Certainly not!

**JEAN-BAPTISTE:**
Well then, I don't understand. The secretary told me . . .

**AGENT:**
Listen, this is a general rule among insurance companies; we consider it a risk to cover any ex-prisoner. We cannot logically register them the same as any ordinary employee in a group insurance plan.

**JEAN-BAPTISTE:**
But you can examine my file, you'll see . . .

**AGENT:**
Let's be logical about this, I have nothing against you personally, but if we had to review each case separately, we'd never finish.

**JEAN-BAPTISTE:**
Well, just who runs the company then, anyway? The owner, or its insurance agents?

AGENT:
We never forced your company to let you go. We simply notified them that we could not assure coverage under the terms of their present contract.

**JEAN-BAPTISTE:**
But, if I understand you correctly, you're kicking me out!

AGENT:
That is not my fault, I am not the one who decides the policies of insurance companies; not even my superior does that, the decisions come from higher up.

**JEAN-BAPTISTE:** *inquisitive*
From who, just exactly?

AGENT:
I have no idea, they come from studies made by computer, from the shareholders, from the man-in-the-street, you and me and the guy next door.

**JEAN-BAPTISTE:**
It seems I've heard that song before, but I have a wife and family. I have as much right as anybody to work.

AGENT:
Young man, you ought to know that insurance companies are not ruled by the democratic system, but by the economic system.

**JEAN-BAPTISTE:**
Well, what do you want me to do then? Kill myself?

**AGENT:**
I never said that.

**JEAN-BAPTISTE:**
Or maybe I should kill the lot of you instead.

*Percussion.*

**CRIER:**
September, 1967.

**14th EMPLOYER:**
Minnesota Chemicals Manufacturing.

**JEAN-BAPTISTE:**
The following June the company closes down and moves to Ontario.

**CRIER:**
June, 1968.

**15th EMPLOYER:**
Top Grade Foods Ltd.

**JEAN-BAPTISTE:**
I'm hired as a foreman.

**CRIER:**
January, 1969.

**JEAN-BAPTISTE:**
I'm fired because I have a criminal record. For more than a year I remain unemployed in spite of a hundred and fifty to a hundred and seventy-five job applications.

**ALL THE JEAN-BAPTISTE M.'s:**

Westinghouse Ltd.
East Central Plumbing Co.
Westmount Realties
Eastern Finance Ltd.
American Standard Oil
British American Oil
American Tools
British Blue Print
Dominion Dry Milks

ALL THE JEAN-BAPTISTE M.'s:

Maple Leaf Bacon
Dominion Glass
Superior Sales
American White Uniforms Ltd.
American Rubber Ltd.
American Window Shades
American Tube and Controls
American Air of Canada Ltd.
DeLuxe Flooring
Simons Mattress

JUDGES:

Don't call us, we'll call you.

JEAN-BAPTISTE:

Discouraged, I register at Reorientation Inc. which helps to find work for ex-cons.

*A JUROR-WITNESS (LOUIS ROBILLARD) comes forward.*

ROBILLARD:

Louis Robillard Executive Director of Reorientation Inc.
Background: Three years – four years – three years concurrent.
Charges: Three counts of armed robbery with violence.
Possession of an illegal weapon with dangerous intent.
Public disturbance – ten shots from a loaded firearm.
Studies: St. Vincent de Paul Penitentiary
Leclerc Institute
Formal Education: 11th grade, general, 11th and 12th grades, sciences, Degree in Social Work.

*He turns around toward JEAN-BAPTISTE.*

**ROBILLARD:**
J.B., I've read your file. You're intelligent, hard working, and your record of offences is minimal. There is no reason that you shouldn't be able to find a job.

**JEAN-BAPTISTE:**
But that's over a hundred applications I've filled out without results.

**ROBILLARD:**
What sort of employment are you looking for?

**JEAN-BAPTISTE:**
Anything, I want to work.

**ROBILLARD:**
Perhaps we may be able to get you in at Dutron.

**JEAN-BAPTISTE:**
The big corporation?

**ROBILLARD:**
Yes, they're very sympathetic to what we're doing here. To tell the truth, without their financial help, we couldn't exist. All our bookkeeping is done at the Dutron offices. You know, thanks to Mr. Stanway, one of their Veeps, we're almost a division of Dutron itself.

**JEAN-BAPTISTE:**
That would be fantastic! A real job! The dream of my life! A job where I could do something useful, where I'd be respected, a job like you see in the movies, with secretaries, and telephones, and elevators . . . a real job! I knew there was justice somewhere; where there's a will, there's a way.

**ROBILLARD:**
Where there's a will, there's a way. Look at me . . . I was a rebel, I figured nobody wanted to give me a chance . . . that it was all the big-shots' fault . . . But once you get to know them, you realize they're just people like you and me, and that all they want is for

**ROBILLARD:**
you to find your place and be assured of the basic necessities. All you need is the will to work.

**JEAN-BAPTISTE:**
Well, I'm willing.

**ROBILLARD:**
And you can . . . Of course, it's not settled yet, you realize. You'll go fill out an application for Dutron, but it will take time. While you're waiting, why don't you drive a taxi for awhile? Fill out an application here!

**CRIER:**
February 12, 1970.

**JEAN-BAPTISTE:**
Inspector-in-Chief, City of Montreal, Department of Licenses.

Dear Sir,
I have been in touch with your office today in order to see what had become of my application. I was advised that my case is still under consideration but that it is possible that a decision may be made in a week's time. I have a family that I wish to keep so that we can make a new life together. I want to be able to hold my head up once again when I walk down the street, is this too much to ask? I wish to work, Sir, most definitely. Sitting here today, I count myself very lucky nevertheless, since I realise that the wrongs which I have committed were considerable. Yes, I am fortunate that society has restored my liberty. But I am ungrateful and selfish, you see, because I am asking something more of society, I am asking you to give me work, allow me to reimburse you for the confidence you have shown in me, yes, Sir, allow me to become a citizen who is a credit to his friends, to his family, and to you, the society.

**THE JURORS:** *writing*

Dear Sir, whatever your decision may be, I will accept it and wish to thank you sincerely for the time and consideration you have devoted to my application.

**JEAN-BAPTISTE:**

Sincerely yours, Jean-Baptiste M.

*Percussion.*

**CRIER:**

March, 1970.

**JUDGES:**

The department of Licenses of the City of Montreal, in a spirit of equity and justice, grants a taxi license to Jean-Baptiste M.

**EVERYBODY:**

Bravo!

*Percussion.*

**JEAN-BAPTISTE:**

I start my job with Yellow Cabs.

**LALONDE, judge:**

Did the accused, in the course of this job, come into contact with disruptive elements of society?

**McPHERSON, judge:**

With anarchists? Communists? Terrorists? Or any other "ists"? . . .

**MARSHALL, judge:**

. . . who may have had an influence on his future, and becoming a determining factor in his behaviour?

**CRIER:**

Let all those who can testify as to the activities of Jean-Baptiste M. come into this circle.

**JUDGES:**

Let each man be free
To speak what he knows
To speak what he thinks
To do what he must
That justice may triumph.

*The JUROR-WITNESSES come out to become taxi-drivers.*

**1st DRIVER:**

If I ever get my hands on that asshole! Fuckin' English bastard just chucked his tip on the floor of my cab, like he was throwin' it to a dog! *He throws a coin on the ground.*

*The JUROR-WITNESSES, in the box, begin to bark, hunting for it on the floor on all fours.*

**2nd DRIVER:**

Answer them in French, that really pisses them off.

**JEAN-BAPTISTE:**

I'm bilingual, aren't you?

**1st DRIVER:**

Sure, sure! But if you can't make yourself understood in your own language, in your own city, you might as well just pack it in and go shovel snow in Ontario . . . in fuckin' August!

**2nd DRIVER:**

It's not enough for them you work sitting on your ass, they wanta see you laid out cold.

**1st DRIVER:**

Hey, this has really been my day! I'm pickin' up a fare at the airport, and lookin' around to back out, I see one of the pigs for the Airport Limousines taking my license number . . .

**3rd DRIVER:**
Tough luck, Froggy, gotta lower your rates!

*The JUROR-WITNESSES, in the panel, call each other down and fight, then stop suddenly.*

**2nd DRIVER:**
It's about time all that changed.

**1st DRIVER:**
Run things our own way, separate. Once and for all, that's what I say.

**JEAN-BAPTISTE:**
Do you believe that?

**1st DRIVER:**
Listen, J.B., before I start driving a taxi I used to think all this talk of colonialism, socialism, separatism, was all just so much bullshit and that was that. Soon as I had a beer in front of me I couldn'ta cared less. But since then, I've come to understand a few things.

**2nd DRIVER:**
Everybody oughta drive a taxi for awhile at least once in their life. It's a lot more educational than goin' to Florida.

**JEAN-BAPTISTE:** *to 1st DRIVER*
What did you learn?

**1st DRIVER:**
Well, we get screwed a lot more than we think. They've got hold of everything, hey, and it's not just the English, it's all our own that are up there workin' with 'em, the guys like you and me. Marryin' them even.

**2nd DRIVER:**
Yeah, everything run by doctors and lawyers. We're not good enough for them. We're slum trash.

**A VOICE:**
Jean-Baptiste M., telephone.

*JEAN-BAPTISTE exits.*

**2nd DRIVER:**
Yeah, everything run by doctors and lawyers. We're not good enough for them. We're slum trash.

**1st DRIVER:**
You coming to the demonstration against Airport Limousine?

**2nd DRIVER:**
No, I don't want to miss Archie Bunker.

**JEAN-BAPTISTE:**
What? Dutron!

**1st DRIVER:**
Christ! No wonder we're not getting anywhere.

**2nd DRIVER:**
Well, you know that I'm for it, but one more or less isn't going to change anything.

**JEAN-BAPTISTE:**
Hey, you guys, it's done! I got it!

**1st DRIVER:**
Got what?

**JEAN-BAPTISTE:**
I got a job with Dutron!

**2nd DRIVER:**
That what you're so excited about?

**JEAN-BAPTISTE:**

Hey, don't you get it? Dutron, one of the biggest companies in the world, that means security for my family, the chance to become somebody! Dutron, that means the best! I told you so!

*Percussion to the rhythm of the lines of all the JEAN-BAPTISTE M.'s. (the Jurors)*

**THE JEAN-BAPTISTE M.'s:**

The greatest chemical empire in the world
Thousands of employees
Dozens of factories
Millions of capital shares
The company that produces:

Kantron nylons
Porlon acrylics
Kraly fibres
Coron rope
Lacron polyesters
Refrigerants, aerosols
Solvents, peroxides
Paints and enamels
Dynamite and other explosives
Frayon
Luco
Lacette
Dulite
Liners

*The enumeration mounts to a crescendo.*

*BLACKOUT*

# Act Two

*The stage is dark. Downstage two SPECTATORS of the trial are waiting to enter the public gallery. One reads a newspaper, the other approaches.*

**1st SPECTATOR:**
You going in to the trial of Mr. What's-His-Name?

**2nd SPECTATOR:**
Yes, you too?

**1st SPECTATOR:**
I wouldn't want to miss it. When she reads the story in the papers, my wife says: "Look, here's a guy that gave up on just talking and actually did it." You see, I've been saying to her every week since God knows when, I'm gonna kill my boss.

**2nd SPECTATOR:**
You agree with his action then?

**1st SPECTATOR:**

Agree, agree, well, let's not exaggerate. I mean, you'd have to have a few screws loose to do a thing like that.

**2nd SPECTATOR:**

They say here though *he points to the newspaper* that the psychiatrist – *he reads* "the prison psychiatrist has established that Jean-Baptiste M. is not suffering from any psychological disorder." Even says he has an above average IQ.

**1st SPECTATOR:**

That must be his problem. As soon as you start thinking and seeing what's going on, and putting the pieces together, you realise there's only two things you can do: shoot yourself or shoot them.

**LAWYER FOR THE DEFENSE:**

It is nevertheless a fact that my client was dismissed from his job. The whole affair had been instigated by an anonymous letter, whose author was never traced. That morning he took the road into town, and on the bridge, the idea of buying a firearm occurred to him. At the store the clerk sold him a .22. He then returned to the plant with the idea of frightening the authorities, still with the same purpose: to get his job back. He waited in the parking lot for M. Guindon to come out, and hoped for a moment that he would be arrested before having time to shoot. I wish to call Dr. Daoust, the prison psychiatrist, to the stand.

*PSYCHIATRIST enters.*

Doctor, can you explain to us the mental state of the accused?

**PSYCHIATRIST:**

The accused is not suffering from any mental disorder, that is absolutely certain.

**LAWYER FOR THE DEFENSE:**
Might he have suffered from any other psychological disturbance?

**PSYCHIATRIST:**
I can only confirm, as I have stated in my report, that for over two years the accused has been visibly obsessed by the loss of his job.

**LAWYER FOR THE DEFENSE:**
Which may have led him to fire on his victim?

**PSYCHIATRIST:**
Yes, to a large degree this obsession has given way to an intense anger, which found an outlet in the gesture in question.

**LAWYER FOR THE DEFENSE:** *turning to the JUDGE*
What I am asking for my client is acquittal, pure and simple. Who could believe that a man who had struggled to regain the position where he felt most useful to society, and where his work was in keeping with his deepest aspirations, who could believe that my client could have deliberately wanted to kill a man, thereby cutting himself off from any chance of realising the dream of his life?

**JUDGE:**
I would like to know how we are to accept the explanation of a sudden, irresistible impulse, when the accused had taken the trouble of purchasing a weapon, loading it, and firing four bullets into the body of the victim, the third shot being fired while the victim lay felled on the pavement? Moreover, how are we to believe, under these circumstances, that he simply wanted to . . . "frighten the authorities"?

**2nd SPECTATOR:**
Incredible, isn't it?

**1st SPECTATOR:**
Yeah, it's that alright!

*Percussion.*

**2nd SPECTATOR:**
Excuse me, it's starting.

*Light up on stage.*

**CRIER:**
The Crown versus Jean-Baptiste M.
For the crime of murder
Upon three counts
For the bereavement
Of three families
Of their means of support
For the willful injury
Of a great enterprise
For disruption
Of the accepted order
On this day of grace
Nineteen hundred and seventy-two
The proceedings will resume –

**JUDGES:**
Let each man be free
To speak what he knows
To speak what he thinks
To do what he must
That justice may triumph.

*Percussion.*

*The desks that were piled on top of one another are now side by side.*

**CRIER:**
April 7, 1970.

**JEAN-BAPTISTE:**
I am hired by the Dutron Co. in the packaging department.

*Percussion.*

**JEAN-BAPTISTE:**

The work I am given is very simple; they have me wrap and send out articles of stationery to the various offices across Canada. Another of my functions if to get old files out of storage when requested. My relations with all the employees are very pleasant and the work is well done.

I am twenty-seven years old, with a wife and one child. I must now provide for my family's future. I find the time goes slowly, I would like to be more useful, to work ten times harder than my job allows me to. When I get home from work at night, Christiane always says to me:

**CHRISTIANE:**

Why can't you just relax, anyway? Put on your slippers, take your tie off. You spend every evening in uniform as if you were expecting to be called by Dutron at any minute.

**JEAN-BAPTISTE:**

It's true, she's right, but it's stronger than I am, I keep my shoes on, I leave on my tie, I am prepared.

*Percussion.*

**CRIER:**

March 15, 1971.

**JEAN-BAPTISTE:**

The company announces its proposal to close down my department.

*D. LALONDE comes in to meet JEAN-BAPTISTE M.*

Monsieur Lalonde, I hear that my department is going to be eliminated as of the first of April!

**LALONDE:**

That's right, but you needn't worry, we'll find you another job to do.

**JEAN-BAPTISTE:**
I'd like to have some more interesting work where I could really help the company.

**LALONDE:**
I can't promise anything.

**JEAN-BAPTISTE:**
I'd rather quit than be put someplace where I had nothing to do.

**LALONDE:**
Well, there is an opening for an inside salesman in the sales department, but I can't promise you anything . . . You speak good English?

**JEAN-BAPTISTE:**
Fluently, sir, I was born in Ottawa.

**LALONDE:**
Do you like the company?

**JEAN-BAPTISTE:**
Yes, sir, very much.

**LALONDE:**
Have you been in the army?

**JEAN-BAPTISTE:**
Yes, sir.

**LALONDE:**
McPherson would like that . . . I'll let you know in a week or two what we can do for you.

**JEAN-BAPTISTE:**
But in two weeks, the department will be shut down already!

**LALONDE:** *excited*
In a week, or two . . .

*Percussion.*

**CRIER:**
March 31.

**JEAN-BAPTISTE:**
I am promoted to inside salesman in the sales department.

*Percussion.*

*Sales Seminar. D. LALONDE rings a bell and the JUROR-WITNESSES make their ways to their seats like children coming into class. Whispering, shoving, schoolroom atmosphere. JEAN-BAPTISTE M. sits down with them, or directly in front of them. At the second ringing of the bell, the group becomes quiet, assuming pupil posture.*

**MARSHALL:**
The company has organised this seminar in order to review some of the essentials of good salesmanship. The seminar will be as useful to our senior employees as to our welcome newer colleagues; such as our most recent member to join the team here: Jean-Baptiste M.

*JEAN-BAPTISTE M. stands up and the others applaud. He sits back down.*

The number-one function of the salesman is to sell his company's product. At each and every encounter he has with his client, he must make a sale.

**McPHERSON:**
In order to live and act positively, and with enthusiasm, you must be proud of your job. You must be convinced that you are an important link in a great chain. The employee, and especially the salesman, who is not wholeheartedly proud of his company, is to be pitied.

**LALONDE:**

Stop thinking of your work as a daily routine, and think of that work as part of a great enterprise which is helping people. Think of your fellow human beings whose lives you are making brighter and less burdensome.

**MARSHALL:**

Consider this example of positive thinking on the part of a salesman: Two salesmen meet and discuss their work. Louis! Emile!

*Two JUROR-WITNESSES leave their benches and come forward to "recite their lesson."*

**1st JUROR:** *irritated*

The better you do, the more they expect! I've increased my sales by ten percent this year and what do you think head office tells me to do?

**2nd JUROR:**

I don't know, what?

**1st JUROR:**

They give me notice my quota's being raised by ten percent! I guess they expected me to thank them!

**2nd JUROR:** *very calmly*

I never argue with head office. I've always found that the quotas they send me are lower than the ones I set for myself.

*The JUROR-WITNESSES applaud while the two actors return to their seats, proud and smiling.*

**MARSHALL:**

Say what you have to say in the simplest possible terms.

**LALONDE:**

Don't talk about yourself, but about "him", the client.

McPHERSON:
Don't leave without his signature at the bottom of the contract.

MARSHALL:
Who has a good example of being concise? *pointing to a JUROR-WITNESS who stands up*

3rd JUROR:
Woodrow Wilson once ended a letter as follows: "Excuse me for having written such a long letter, but I didn't have time to write you a shorter one."

MARSHALL: *points to another JUROR who stand up*
Anybody else?

4th JUROR:
Two thousand years ago, Julius Caesar described his triumphant adventure in Gaul in three words: "veni, vidi, vici".

THE OTHERS: *in chorus*
Huh? What?

4th JUROR:
I came, I saw, I conquered.

McPHERSON:
We live in a universe of laws; man regulates the world and causes it to act in his own interest by patiently uncovering those laws, and then by respecting them; the more he respects them, the better he lives, and in living according to the laws, he lives with confidence.

LALONDE:
This applies to each one of us here at the company, in our personal lives and in our work. The man who lives by the law learns to love the law he lives by, and lives without fear.

MARSHALL:
Now, what do we have next on the agenda?

*The JUROR-WITNESSES call out for the classic annual baseball scene.*

1st JUROR:
Jimmy, you're a great ball player, in fact, you're one of the top stars of the New York Yankees.

2nd JUROR:
That's right, Mr. McCarthy.

1st JUROR:
You're young, you're hitting .350, you're great in the field . . . I'm going to miss you.

2nd JUROR: *dumbfounded*
. . . miss me?

1st JUROR:
I gave you an order yesterday, and you ignored it. That was the third time that's happened.

2nd JUROR:
But . . . I'm a good player! . . .

1st JUROR:
The team is gonna miss you, you're shippin' out tomorrow. *He holds out his hand.* Good luck, Jimmy boy, and for God sake get it through your head you're not as hot as you think you are!

*Applause. The pupils make stadium crowd noises . . . MARSHALL restores order with the bell.*

MARSHALL: *faster now*
A salesman's goals are:

1st JUROR:
To get new orders.

2nd JUROR:
To get back former clients.

3rd JUROR:
To increase volume of sales.

4th JUROR:
To hold on to present clients.

MARSHALL:
The reasons for calling a client are:

5th JUROR:
To get acquainted.

6th JUROR:
To obtain information.

1st JUROR:
To be of service.

2nd JUROR:
To sell.

*The JUROR-WITNESSES drum with pencils and hands, for this enumeration, which turns into a kind of "concert". The music of the beginning of the scene plays under it softly.*

LALONDE:
The things you should know about your client are:

McPHERSON:
With regard to your client's personnel:

1st JUROR:
Organization of client's company.

2nd JUROR:
Decision makers.

3rd JUROR:
Decision influencers.

4th JUROR:
Employee promotions, transfers, retirements . . . *etc.*

5th JUROR:
Political climate between individuals, departments, sections, floors . . . *etc.*

6th JUROR:
Their feelings towards you, towards your competition.

1st JUROR:
Ambitions of individuals you are acquainted with.

2nd JUROR:
Personal likes, dislikes and prejudices of these persons.

3rd JUROR:
Their background and experience.

McPHERSON:
With regard to your client's product!

LALONDE:
Production problems.

1st JUROR:
Quality problems.

2nd JUROR:
Marketing problems: size and growth potential.

3rd JUROR:
Research and development services.

4th JUROR:
Selling forces to which client has access.

5th JUROR:
How client's finished product is made and sold.

6th JUROR:
Profitability or return on investment.

1st JUROR:
What benefits client expects of your product.

McPHERSON:
With regard to the client's company:

LALONDE:
Goals of the company.

1st JUROR:
Size and assets of company.

2nd JUROR:
Image employees have of the company.

3rd JUROR:
Image company is trying to convey to the public.

4th JUROR:
Stock value.

5th JUROR:
The company's credit.

MARSHALL:
Ours is a civilisation of technology. We turn wheels and wheels and wheels within wheels. They don't turn just for the sake of turning. They turn to produce what men can use and enjoy. What makes the machine great is that it serves man.

*Applause. The class appears to want to leave. MARSHALL quiets them down again.*

I hope that you will give some thought to the various ideas we have examined in this seminar, because they form not only a guide to salesmanship, but a guide to all our human relationships as well: They hold true for friendships; they hold true for marital life; they hold

**MARSHALL:**

true for good family life. And as you go back to your work, I'd like you to remember something that Lord Chesterfield once said to his son, "My boy, make other people like themselves just a little bit better, and I promise you this – they will like you very much."

*The JUROR-WITNESSES applaud.*

**CRIER:**

First week of April.

**JEAN-BAPTISTE:**

I've started work in the sales department. Right from the first week I feel a difficulty in communication with Mr. Marshall. Marshall is the paternal type, a bit of a schoolmaster. He thinks everything should go through him, even the petty day to day problems.

*Percussion.*

**CRIER:**

Second week of April.

**JEAN-BAPTISTE:**

I had hoped that the situation would improve. That hasn't been the case. I'm the type who likes to feel a sense of satisfaction at having accomplished something. With Marshall, it's impossible. I feel useless around him. I'm trapped in a job where I can't make decisions, can't ask questions, can't feel a sense of responsibility or participation.

*Percussion.*

**CRIER:**

Third week of April.

**JEAN-BAPTISTE:**

Maybe it's my fault, they don't know me well enough yet. I decided to assert myself, I question, I suggest, I try to help. When I'm not in agreement with Marshall, I immediately assure him that I intervened only with the intention of being more efficient and more useful and that this can only benefit the company.

*Link.*

*A JUROR-WITNESS on the phone.*

**CLIENT:**

Hello, Dutron? This is Larue Construction Incorporated. I'm calling about my order.

**JEAN-BAPTISTE:**

Could you give me your P.O. number?

**CLIENT:**

3785-625.

**JEAN-BAPTISTE:**

3785-625. And your S.O. number?

**CLIENT:**

I don't know.

**JEAN-BAPTISTE:**

Do you have your acknowledgement slip?

**CLIENT:**

Yes.

**JEAN-BAPTISTE:**

At the top, on the left.

**CLIENT:**

Yes, S.O. 132753.

**JEAN-BAPTISTE:**

I'll check into it.

**CLIENT:**

You'd better do more than check into it! I was promised delivery on the 22nd and this is the 27th. I've got fifteen men here that I'm paying to sit and twiddle their thumbs. And the plumber and electrician are breathing down our necks!

**JEAN-BAPTISTE:**

Hold the line, I'll see what I can do. *He pushes a button and dials another number.* Sales processing.

*A JUROR-WITNESS answers.*

**SWITCHBOARD GIRL:**

Sales processing, one moment please.

**2nd JUROR:**

Sales processing, Pierre Labonte.

**JEAN-BAPTISTE:**

Hello, Pierre, I'm calling about the delivery of our S.O. 132753 for Larue Construction, P.O. 3785-625.

**2nd JUROR:**

You know the regulation, you have to send me a request for delivery dates.

**JEAN-BAPTISTE:**

But it's five days late. It was due on the 22nd.

**2nd JUROR:**

Then you're supposed to send me a "Late Delivery Tracer."

**JEAN-BAPTISTE:**

He's got fifteen men waiting on the job! Give it a try, eh!

2nd JUROR:

I'll see if I can make out a special, but I'm not promising anything. *He dials a number.* Shipping department.

SWITCHBOARD GIRL:

Shipping department, one moment please.

3rd JUROR:

Shipping department, Normand Houle.

2nd JUROR:

Normand, Pierre in Sales Processing. You wouldn't have shipment for Larue Construction, S.O. 132753, would you?

3rd JUROR:

No, I haven't got anything.

2nd JUROR:

O.K. Thanks. *He dials another number.* Credit department.

SWITCHBOARD GIRL:

Credit department, one moment please.

4th JUROR:

Credit department, Roy Barney.

2nd JUROR:

Hello, Roy, this is Pierre. Have you, by any chance, a hold up on S.O. 132753 for Larue Construction?

4th JUROR:

I don't think so, but I can't tell, send me a request.

2nd JUROR:

But there's fifteen people on the job site waiting for the goods.

**4th JUROR:**
Sorry, old boy, all I can do is check but it will take time. Why don't you call shipping?

**2nd JUROR:**
I did.

**4th JUROR:**
Anyway, these people at sales are pushing as if they were the only important persons in the organisation.

**2nd JUROR:**
Yes, I know, but could you check?

**4th JUROR:**
I'll try, I'll call you back.

**2nd JUROR:**
Before 3?

**4th JUROR:**
I'll try. *He dials another number.*

**2nd JUROR:**
Production department.

**SWITCHBOARD GIRL:** *perhaps a little exasperated*
Just a minute please.

**5th JUROR:**
Production department, Mark speaking.

**2nd JUROR:**
This is Pierre at Sales processing. I'm looking for S.O. 132753 for Larue Construction.

**5th JUROR:**
Send a request.

**2nd JUROR:**
But it is an emergency.

5th JUROR:

I'll try to find out, but I won't promise any results.

*The JUROR-WITNESSES telephone each other, by means of the switchboard operators:*

JUROR-WITNESSES:

5th Juror to 3rd Juror: S.O. 132753
3rd Juror to 4th Juror: S.O. 132753
4th Juror to 5th Juror: S.O. 132753
5th Juror to Jean-Baptiste: S.O. 132753 . . . *etc.*

JEAN-BAPTISTE: *to CLIENT*

Can I call you back? We are tracing your order.

*The CLIENT hangs up violently, dials another number. MARSHALL answers.*

CLIENT:

This is Larue Construction, I was promised delivery on the 22nd. I have 15 people waiting on the job. If you don't give me an answer within 15 minutes on when I can expect my equipment, I won't place another order with your firm.

MARSHALL:

You will get your answer, Mr. Larue, would you please hold the line. *MARSHALL goes over to JEAN-BAPTISTE.* What's the score on this Larue Construction business?

JEAN-BAPTISTE:

They want their equipment as soon as possible. We're tracing their order, I'm taking care of it.

MARSHALL:

Yes, but you don't have to go disrupting the whole company for one order.

JEAN-BAPTISTE:

Well, what should I have done?

MARSHALL:

Told him that his equipment had been sent by mistake to Seven Islands. In the first place, you'd have been able to stall for time. In the second place, you would have had a chance to write out a request for late delivery. In the third place, you'd have been sure not to lose the sale.

JEAN-BAPTISTE:

I think I can find a better solution.

MARSHALL:

I'm not asking for your opinion.

JEAN-BAPTISTE:

O.K., fine, fine. I'll call him back then.

MARSHALL:

Never mind, I've got him waiting on the line now.

*MARSHALL grabs the phone out of J.B.M.'s hands.*

Roy Marshall speaking, give me Sales processing, Shipping department, Production, Engineering.

THE FIVE JURORS:

Sales Processing.
Shipping department.
Credit department.
Production department.
Engineering department.

MARSHALL:

This is Marshall at sales. I want an answer on S.O. 132753 at once. S.O. 132753.

THE FIVE JURORS:

Not here.
No answer yet.
Held up for technicality.
Being processed for shipment for tomorrow morning.
Already processed.

*MARSHALL resumes his communication with the CLIENT.*

**MARSHALL:**
Mr. Larue, I am sorry to have kept you waiting so long: shipment will be made tomorrow morning.

**CLIENT:**
Thank you.

**MARSHALL:** *to JEAN-BAPTISTE*
Why didn't you send out a tracer?

**JEAN-BAPTISTE:**
But that would have taken two days to get an answer.

**MARSHALL:**
You're not being asked to think, but to follow the regulations. The important thing isn't the results, it's keeping all the cogs in the machine well-oiled. The men that designed the regulations were paid for it, and you're being paid to follow them.

*JEAN-BAPTISTE comes downstage, he addresses the audience.*

*The JUROR-WITNESSES are dimly lit and are recreating an office atmosphere: telephones, typewriter, filing, coffees, etc. As the monologue progresses their movements become increasingly inhuman.*

*Percussion.*

**CRIER:**
Fourth week of April.

**JEAN-BAPTISTE:**
It is difficult, but I put my whole heart into my work. I made a special effort to find means of making my duties simpler. I ask for, and receive supplementary work.

*Percussion.*

**CRIER:**
First week of May.

**JEAN-BAPTISTE:**
Despite all my efforts, I am reduced to doing a routine job and to reacting like a machine. Is my work satisfactory? I've never had any criticisms, on the contrary, I have even had compliments on my work.

*Percussion.*

**CRIER:**
Second week of May.

**JEAN-BAPTISTE:**
I am sick of being treated like a robot by the company, by my bosses Marshall and Lalonde. I get more and more discouraged, and even think about quitting my job. I decide to stay because I have hope that any work can become more human, and because I want to make myself a career with Dutron. Nevertheless I get more and more depressed. I feel as if I'm no longer alive, and that my movements are automatic. Sunday nights are the worst; I think about the week ahead . . . I'm no use to anybody or anything, and yet I could do so much . . . so much . . .

*Percussion.*

**CRIER:**
Sunday, May 15.

**JEAN-BAPTISTE:**
I swallow a hundred tranquillizers.

**JUDGES:**
Let all those who can testify to the actions of Jean-Baptiste M. come into this circle.

**JUDGES:**

Let each man be free
To speak what he knows
To speak what he thinks
To do what he must
That justice may triumph.

*A JUROR – CHRISTIANE come forward to be with JEAN-BAPTISTE, who is lying down.*

**CHRISTIANE:**

The doctor's left. I called Robillard, he's coming over.

**JEAN-BAPTISTE:** *delirious*

Mam, I'll succeed, you know. The army was the only time I ever made a mockery out of work. I thought then that when you were working, you didn't have to stop living.

**MOTHER–JUROR:**

It's all right, Jean-Baptiste.

**JEAN-BAPTISTE:**

Christiane.

**CHRISTIANE:**

Yes?

**JEAN-BAPTISTE:**

It was prison . . . You know, if I hadn't gone to prison, I could have been Prime Minister.

**CHRISTIANE:**

Yes, Jean-Baptiste, just rest; Robillard's coming over.

**JEAN-BAPTISTE:**

I'm going to wear your boots someday. I'm going to have a wife and kids too, and a house and furniture and a car. I'm going to be a man; I'm healthy, I'm intelligent, I know how to read, write and count, I speak good English, I'm brave, I like people, I'm honest, and I'm going to be happy. I'm going to be somebody.

*JEAN-BAPTISTE dozes off towards the end of his speech.*

*A JUROR-WITNESS, comes downstage: LOUIS ROBILLARD. ROBILLARD approaches the couple.*

**ROBILLARD:**
Did the doctor see him?

**CHRISTIANE:**
Yes, it's not serious, he just needs to rest.

**ROBILLARD:**
Why did he do it?

**CHRISTIANE:**
I've no idea.

**ROBILLARD:**
Are things going well between you?

**CHRISTIANE:**
We've always got along well, Mr. Robillard, and we still do.

**ROBILLARD:**
This is awful, he's going to mess up everything; Dutron is our ally, financially and morally.

**CHRISTIANE:**
This has nothing to do with Dutron, what matters is Jean-Baptiste.

**ROBILLARD:**
Dutron matters too; if we lose their confidence, what's going to become of us? We're all in the same boat, Christiane, and we have to help each other out.

CHRISTIANE:

No, we're not in the same boat! All you're thinking about is Dutron; I'm thinking of Jean-Baptiste. And Jean-Baptiste I understand.

ROBILLARD:

You work hard yourself, and yet you don't pull stunts like this.

CHRISTIANE:

That's not the same thing. I'm a woman. We've been prepared for it. A woman doesn't have thirty-seven different careers to choose from . . . She can either fight the household dirt battle with one eye on the Newlywed Game, or else she can join the steno pool. Myself, I've got the best of both worlds, I get to type and dust both, right in the office, and listen to the hit parade on the Muzak. I answer the phone, I hunt up files, I correct letters, I type letters, I do bugger-all. But it's no strain on me, I'm in great shape. Jean-Baptiste is a man, for him it's not the same thing.

ROBILLARD:

Come on now, let's not exaggerate. Thousands of people do what he does and are no worse for it.

CHRISTIANE:

One of these days he's going to get angry.

ROBILLARD:

I got angry once myself; I got three years – four years – three years concurrent. That didn't stop me from beginning a new life and being useful.

CHRISTIANE:

I have nothing against you, Mr. Robillard, you do your best, you patch things up . . . But Jean-Baptiste is a guy who's all in one piece, when he believes in something, he believes in it with a passion. He married me and loves me with a passion and if I were to cheat on him, he'd kill me. You've persuaded him to love society, and now he loves it with a passion.

*JEAN-BAPTISTE comes out of his stupor. He talks slowly and with difficulty.*

**JEAN-BAPTISTE:**
Mr. Marshall, we ought to check on whether we have any Kantron in stock, and

any Porlon
any Kraly
any Coron
any Lacron
any Teflon
any Aerosol
any Luco
any Dulite
any Explosives

**ROBILLARD:**
J.B., hey! J.B., it's me, Louis! Louis Robillard.

**JEAN-BAPTISTE:**
Louis? . . . Louis, is that you?

**ROBILLARD:**
Yes, me, J.B., feeling any better?

**JEAN-BAPTISTE:**
No, nothing's any better, it's all rotten . . . Christiane! Where is Christiane?

**CHRISTIANE:**
I'm here, don't worry, I'll make you some coffee.

**ROBILLARD:**
Come on, J.B., you've got to perk up a bit.

**JEAN-BAPTISTE:**
I've had it, ten hours a day, going around in circles, I'm just goddam fed up.

ROBILLARD:

You can't just let yourself go, you've got fantastic potential, you're one helluva guy.

JEAN-BAPTISTE: *laughs with difficulty*

A helluva guy! I can't even make a decision . . . eh! I'm almost thirty years old and I can't even make a decision. *weak*

ROBILLARD:

In any activity there are going to be problems . . .

JEAN-BAPTISTE:

Well I'm going to make a decision; I'm going to load my gun, and I'm going to shoot myself.

ROBILLARD:

Stop that, J.B.! Your responsibility is to spread love around you, to enjoy the satisfaction of a duty well done, to make your family and your friends happy. Happiness is a lot of little things, and I'm sure you're capable, J.B.

JEAN-BAPTISTE:

I'm going to load my gun . . .

ROBILLARD:

Listen! You possess some wonderful qualities, and you have a great talent for using them. Have I ever lied to you? If you sow well, then you'll reap well.

JEAN-BAPTISTE:

It's all very nice what you say, Louis, but with the system, the way it is . . . there's only one way out. *He points to his gun.* And this is it.

*ROBILLARD takes the gun out of JEAN-BAPTISTE's hands.*

Give it back to me, Louis. *urgently:* Louis.

**ROBILLARD**: *looks at the rifle, feels it, and suddenly pulls out the breech.*

*JEAN-BAPTISTE screams, reaching for his groin as if being castrated.*

There, it's done . . . Take it easy, J.B., it's for your own good. You'll see, you'll thank me for it.

**JEAN-BAPTISTE**: *sobbing*
They all say the same thing, you're just like them.

**ROBILLARD**:
No, no, J.B., look here, I'm your friend.

*JEAN-BAPTISTE sobs, CHRISTIANE runs in.*

**CHRISTIANE**:
What's the matter?

**ROBILLARD**:
I removed the breech, a simple precaution . . .

*CHRISTIANE consoles JEAN-BAPTISTE.*

I'll put it in a safe place for a few days and I'll give it back when you're feeling better.

*Percussion.*

**CRIER**:
May 16, nine o'clock.

*COLE STANWAY calls on McPHERSON and MARSHALL.*

**STANWAY**:
Hello, Doug, could you get Jean-Baptiste M. up here?

**McPHERSON**:
He's not here, Mr. Stanway, he's been sick the last three days.

**STANWAY:**
Nothing serious?

**McPHERSON:**
No, he phoned in. He'll be back tomorrow.

**STANWAY:**
I wanted to tell him we've chosen him to take an improvement course. He'll have two week-long sessions, in August and in November.

**McPHERSON:**
I'll tell him tomorrow. *to MARSHALL* I didn't know you had to be an ex-con to get ahead at Dutron.

*COLE STANWAY leaves McPHERSON who talks to MARSHALL.*

*ROBILLARD comes to see STANWAY.*

**ROBILLARD:**
Excuse me for bothering you, Mr. Stanway, but I'd like to ask you to keep this object in the lockers you gave us.

**STANWAY:**
What is it?

**ROBILLARD:**
The breech of Jean-Baptiste M.'s rifle. He's going through a bit of a depression, and I just thought I'd take a few precautions.

**STANWAY:**
I'll have it taken down to Blanchet.

**ROBILLARD:**
Thank you. *ROBILLARD leaves.*

**STANWAY:** *to his SECRETARY*
Take this down to Blanchet and ask him to put it in with Reorientation's files.

**1st SECRETARY:**
Yes, sir. *She leaves and meets another SECRETARY.*

**2nd SECRETARY:**
What have you got there?

**1st SECRETARY:**
I don't know. It belongs to J.B.

**2nd SECRETARY:**
That guy in Sales processing who's always asking for extra work?

**1st SECRETARY:**
That's him, the one that wants to explain to everybody how they should work.

**2nd SECRETARY:**
To listen to him, half the staff ought to be fired.

**1st SECRETARY:**
Don't even talk about things like that.

**2nd SECRETARY:**
Wait! Let's show it to the others!

*The employees gather around the SECRETARY, as at coffee break. Lively talk, laughter. They pass around the breech which ends up in the hands of LALONDE who has just arrived.*

**LALONDE:**
The breech from a 410!

*The employees quickly pass the breech around again in silence. The breech ends up in the hands of JEAN-BAPTISTE.*

*Percussion.*

**JEAN-BAPTISTE:**

I go back to work. I attend, with success, the management by objectives course. For four months I apply myself to give full satisfaction. I realize that my superiors are terribly incompetent and that they are doing nothing to improve their contacts. I try to instigate more efficiency in the functions of the department, at the same time avoiding any open clash with my superiors. In the evenings I often think about the way things ought to work for the good of the company. Most likely it is these preoccupations which cause me to eat little and sleep less and less. *JEAN-BAPTISTE makes a phone call.*

*In contrast to the scene with Larue Construction, this one is played calmly, with precision.*

Sales processing.

**SECRETARY:**

Sales processing.

**PIERRE LABONTE:**

Sales processing. Pierre Labonte.

**JEAN-BAPTISTE:**

Hello, Pierre, J.B. here, I'd like to put a hold on twenty pounds of Cralon for the week of the 11th.

**PIERRE LABONTE:**

You'll have to check with production. If it's O.K., then you can send me a requisition write up.

*All the JURORS are in place.*

**1st WOMAN:**

A big strong boy like him, he'll be a fireman.

**1st MAN:**

Or a policeman.

**3rd WOMAN:**
Or an M.P.

**2nd MAN:**
He looks bright, he'll be a teacher.

**1st WOMAN:**
In any case, he's a man.

**JEAN-BAPTISTE:** *telephones*
Production department.

**SECRETARY:**
One moment please.

**MARK:**
Production department, Mark speaking.

**JEAN-BAPTISTE:**
Mark, J.B. here, I'd like to hold twenty pounds of Kralon, for delivery on the week of the 11th.

**MARK:**
It could be done, but you have to write a requisition.

**JEAN-BAPTISTE:**
I'm doing that now.

**MARK:**
I also need a clearance from your superior.

**JEAN-BAPTISTE:**
O.K., I will see Roy Marshall. *JEAN-BAPTISTE stands up, turns towards MARSHALL's office, and freezes.*

**ONE OF THE JURORS:**
I'm going to wear your boots one of these days. I'm intelligent, I know how to write, read, count, I speak good English, I'm going to become somebody, this is a free country, everybody has an equal chance, anybody can become Prime Minister.

*JEAN-BAPTISTE goes into MARSHALL's office.*

JEAN-BAPTISTE:
Mr. Marshall, I want to hold twenty pounds of Kralon for Dominion Textiles for the week of the 11th.

MARSHALL:
Call sales processing.

JEAN-BAPTISTE:
It's done.

MARSHALL:
Call production.

JEAN-BAPTISTE:
It's done.

MARSHALL:
Make out a requisition write-up.

JEAN-BAPTISTE:
I've got it here, but I need your O.K.

MARSHALL:
Have you called the credit department?

JEAN-BAPTISTE:
But Dominion Textile's credit is unquestionable. They could buy millions of pounds without having to have their credit checked out.

MARSHALL:
Call credit!

JEAN-BAPTISTE:
They're bigger than Dutron!

MARSHALL:
Call credit, is that clear?

1st MANAGER:

As far as I'm concerned, there's only one thing that counts, and that's the goal. And to that end, the employee must respect the directions of the company. And it wasn't me who issued those directives. They were communicated to me through the district manager.

5th MANAGER:

And it wasn't him that made them up.

2nd MANAGER:

He received them from the marketing director.

4th MANAGER:

Who, in turn, received them from the general manager.

1st MANAGER:

Who, in turn, receives them from the board of directors who obtained them from a management counselling firm.

2nd MANAGER:

And the board is responsible to the wishes of the shareholders.

4th MANAGER:

And the shareholders are everybody, the man in the street; you and me and the guy next door!

JEAN-BAPTISTE: *on phone*

Credit department.

SECRETARY:

Credit department, one moment please.

ROY BARNEY:

Credit department, Roy Barney.

JEAN-BAPTISTE:

Roy, could you clear an order from Dominion Textiles for twenty pounds of Kralon.

ROY BARNEY:

Twenty pounds! Dominion Textiles' credit is good for twenty thousand.

JEAN-BAPTISTE:

That's what I thought.

ROY BARNEY:

But, you have to send me an inter-office memo, I'll put my O.K. on it.

JEAN-BAPTISTE:

But Roy, I'm going to lose another two days.

ROY BARNEY:

I need the memo. Sorry, J.B.

ALL THE JURORS:

*Their calling begins very softly and then builds to a crescendo.*

J.B. . . . J.B. . . . here J.B. . . . faster J.B. come here J.B. . . . come here . . .

*Percussion which halts the action.*

CRIER:

Montreal
Wednesday, October 6,
Eve of the tragedy.
Let all those who can testify to the actions of
Jean-Baptiste M. come into this circle.

JUDGES:

Let each man be free
To speak what he knows
To speak what he thinks
To do what he must
That justice may triumph.

**JEAN-BAPTISTE:**
Hello, Mr. Lambert, please.

**SECRETARY:**
I'm sorry, Mr. Lambert is not in.

**JEAN-BAPTISTE:**
This is Jean-Baptiste from the Sales department. I'm sick, I'm going to stay home today.

**SECRETARY:**
Anything serious?

**JEAN-BAPTISTE:**
No, just indigestion.

**SECRETARY:**
All right, I'll notify your superiors.

*The JUROR-WITNESS Lemay goes to talk to MARSHALL who talks to McPHERSON and LALONDE.*

*Lemay whispers to MARSHALL.*

*MARSHALL goes to find McPHERSON and LALONDE.*

J.B. is sick, he won't be in today.

**MARSHALL:**
Don't tell me he's going through another depression!

**LALONDE:**
What depression?

**McPHERSON:**
Didn't you hear about it?

**MARSHALL:**
He swallowed a hundred pills, even wanted to put a bullet through his head.

LALONDE:

What? Say, that'd make us look good. Dutron drives its employees to suicide. Some headline that'd be.

MARSHALL:

Unless he's staying home to work on another report on "How Dutron ought to be run."

McPHERSON:

His ideas aren't completely stupid, but they'd require a total reorganization. I did work over a few of his points though for my annual report.

LALONDE:

This suicide story is outrageous.

MARSHALL:

And he's an ex-con at that; one of Stanway's proteges.

McPHERSON:

Yes, that is a risk.

MARSHALL:

And he's always disputing something.

LALONDE: *to MARSHALL*

Well, what are you waiting for?

McPHERSON: *also turning towards MARSHALL*

Well, what are you waiting for?

MARSHALL:

That's all I ask, gentlemen.

LALONDE:

Well, take advantage of this and settle it right now.

*Silence.*

**McPHERSON:**
But the reason . . .

**MARSHALL:**
The reason, I'll take care of the reason.

**McPHERSON:**
Perfect!

**LALONDE:**
Done.

**MARSHALL:**
Right away?

**LALONDE:**
Of course, right away, there's plenty more fish in the pond he came from.

*They laugh.*

*MARSHALL picks up the phone, dials a number. Ringing.*

*M. and all the JUROR-WITNESSES pick up receivers.*

**MARSHALL:**
Hello, M.?

**ALL THE M.'s:**
Yes.

**MARSHALL:**
Roy Marshall here, you're fired.

**1st M.:**
Fired!

**2nd M.:**
That's impossible!

3rd M.:

But I haven't done anything wrong.

4th M.:

I need to work.

5th M.:

This is a joke!

MARSHALL:

It's no joke, it's quite serious.

JEAN-BAPTISTE:

For what reason?

MARSHALL:

Insubordination.

JEAN-BAPTISTE:

That's impossible! We've always had a good relationship.

1st M.:

I've always done my best.

2nd M.:

I've never been impolite.

3rd M.:

I've always given everything I could.

4th M.:

I've always been on time.

5th M.:

I've always followed instructions.

MARSHALL:

It's already decided.

JEAN-BAPTISTE:

But I have a family to support.

1st M.:

I have a wife and child.

2nd M.:

You can't fire me like this on the phone.

MARSHALL:

If you want to know more about it, call Mr. McPherson. *pause*

JEAN-BAPTISTE:

All right, I'm coming in to pick up my personal things.

MARSHALL:

No! Don't bother, we'll mail them to you. *He hangs up.*

*All the M.'s hang up, totally dumfounded.*

JEAN-BAPTISTE:

It just isn't possible!

1st M.:

A company like Dutron can't act like that.

2nd M.:

If a company like Dutron acts like that, then nothing makes sense anymore.

3rd M.:

What am I going to do?

4th M.:

What's going to become of me?

5th M.:

I'm sick and tired of always fighting to be accepted.

**JEAN-BAPTISTE:**
I'm sick and tired of always getting shot down.

*A JUROR-WITNESS – CHRISTIANE comes downstage.*

*All the JUROR-WITNESSES come to join JEAN-BAPTISTE M. who paces back and forth.*

Christiane, I've been fired.

**CHRISTIANE:**
They didn't! Why?

**1st M.:**
I don't know; they said insubordination.

**2nd M.:**
Why would they do that Christiane?

**3rd M.:**
I always did what they wanted me to.

**4th M.:**
I never raised my voice.

**5th M.:**
I tried to help them every way I could.

**1st M.:**
I didn't ask for anything.

**2nd M.:**
Just my job security.

**3rd M.:**
To be able to raise my son.

**4th M.:**
To give him a bit of help.

**5th M.:**
To try to be happy.

**JEAN-BAPTISTE:**
Why did they deceive me, Christiane?

**CHRISTIANE:**
They didn't deceive you, Jean-Baptiste, they've always been like that . . . You deceived yourself, Jean-Baptiste, thinking they considered you a man.

**ALL THE M.'s:**
They were the ones that deceived me.

**CHRISTIANE:**
No! Don't believe that, Jean-Baptiste, forget all that. Things'll work out, you'll find something else.

**1st M.:**
I can't go crawling on my knees any longer.

**2nd M.:**
For them to allow me to earn a living.

**3rd M.:**
To have the right to look you in the eye.

**4th M.:**
I don't want to be a shadow anymore.

**5th M.:**
Or a sheep.

**JEAN-BAPTISTE:**
I don't want to have to send my son away and go begging for handouts.

**1st M.:**
Having to explain to them . . .

**2nd M.:**
That I haven't done anything . . .

**3rd M.:**

That I'm a man.

**4th M.:**

If life is always going to be like this, I'll never be happy.

**5th M.:**

I've waited such a long time to be happy.

**JEAN-BAPTISTE:**

To go on like this isn't living, it's just surviving. *He calls McPHERSON.* Mr. McPherson, this is Jean-Baptiste M.

**1st M.:**

Roy Barney.

**2nd M.:**

Jean Gagnon.

**3rd M.:**

Agathe Marchand.

**4th M.:**

Jeanine Peloquin.

**5th M.:**

Roger Lemieux.

**6th M.:**

Normand Houle.

**7th M.:**

Pierre Labonte.

**JEAN-BAPTISTE:**

Have you been informed about my firing?

**McPHERSON:**

Yes.

**JEAN-BAPTISTE:**
I can't understand the reason for it.

**McPHERSON:**
Marshall spoke to Lalonde about you and they decided to dismiss you immediately. I gave them authorization.

**JEAN-BAPTISTE:**
It's unfair to make a decision like that without taking into consideration all points of view.

**ALL THE M.'s:**
Yes, it's unfair.

**McPHERSON:**
Young man, you will realise someday that industry is not a democratic system and does not have to answer to anybody.

**JEAN-BAPTISTE:**
I want to be granted at least the right to defend myself, whatever the reason.

**McPHERSON:**
Very well! Tomorrow at nine o'clock, in my office.

**JEAN-BAPTISTE:**
Thank you.

*McPHERSON hangs up bruskly.*

**ALL THE M.'s:**
Thank you, thank you, thank you.

**CHRISTIANE:**
Take it easy, Jean-Baptiste, you might be able to get an explanation from the bosses.

**1st M.:**
I don't believe it.

**2nd M.:**
It'd be useless anyway.

**JEAN-BAPTISTE:** *very calmly*
You must be tired, go get some rest.

**CHRISTIANE:**
You won't do anything stupid!

**JEAN-BAPTISTE:**
No, it's over, I'm perfectly calm now.

*CHRISTIANE goes back to the juror-witnesses bench.*

*M. picks up his rifle and saws off the barrel.*

If I can't get myself hired back on, I'll put a bullet through my head right in front of them.

**1st M.:**
It's the only solution.

**2nd M.:**
We are employees.

**3rd M.:**
We either obey, or we disappear.

**4th M.:**
It is the only solution.

**5th M.:**
We either obey, or we disappear.

*Percussion.*

**CRIER:**
Thursday, the 7th of October.

*The JUROR-WITNESSES consult their watches. They show signs of impatience.*

*M. fits his sawed-off rifle into a small briefcase.*

*A JUROR-WITNESS – CHRISTIANE comes to join M.*

CHRISTIANE:
Are you sure you don't want any breakfast?

JEAN-BAPTISTE:
No, I'm not hungry. Anyway I'll grab something in the cafeteria before I go up.

CHRISTIANE:
What time is your appointment with McPherson?

JEAN-BAPTISTE:
Nine o'clock.

CHRISTIANE:
I'm sure they'll listen to you. It'll work out, it has to work out.

JEAN-BAPTISTE:
We'll see, it's time to get going, you're going to be late.

CHRISTIANE:
Yes, you're right, life goes on.

*Percussion.*

CRIER:
Thursday, October 7, 8:20 a.m.

*Percussion.*

JEAN-BAPTISTE:
I looked through my drawers, all my personal effects had been removed from my desk. That disappointed me, very much.

*Percussion.*

**CRIER:**
Eight-thirty.

*Percussion.*

*A JUROR-WITNESS comes downstage.*

Mr. Stanway!

*STANWAY notices M. and acknowledges him with a little wave of the hand, but remains where he is. M. goes over to him hurriedly. STANWAY is visibly uncomfortable at seeing him.*

Mr. Stanway, it's good to see you.

**STANWAY:**
Same here!

**JEAN-BAPTISTE:**
Do you know I've been fired?

**STANWAY:**
I heard something vaguely to that effect.

**JEAN-BAPTISTE:**
I don't understand it; if they'd at least tell me why. I've always worked as hard as I could.

**STANWAY:**
I'm not familiar with the details. You know how it is. Husbands and bosses are always the last to find out.

**JEAN-BAPTISTE:**
I know to what extent you've always been honest with me, and I want to be honest with you; I need this job, not just for the salary, but to show the world I'm good for something, it's that important to me!

**STANWAY:**
Now, now, J.B., it's nothing to get so excited about, you're young and intelligent. Where there's a will, there's a way. You've got your whole life ahead of you.

**JEAN-BAPTISTE:**
What life?

**STANWAY:** *trying to get away*
And besides, you're getting a chance to explain yourself to Mr. McPherson.

**JEAN-BAPTISTE:**
Ah, you do know the details?

**STANWAY:**
Vaguely, very vaguely . . . but I must run now, lot of important appointments, lot of decisions waiting for me.

**JEAN-BAPTISTE:** *knowingly*
Yes, I understand.

**STANWAY:**
Well, good luck then, and don't take it all so tragically.
*He goes off, leaving M. alone.*

**JEAN-BAPTISTE:**
What did he say to me? He didn't say anything! . . . "Don't take it all so tragically", sure, it's no tragedy for him.

**ALL THE M.'s:**
Guys like me, there's thousands of them, too many in fact.

*Percussion.*

**CRIER:**
Eight forty five.

**JEAN-BAPTISTE:**
I show up at McPherson's office.

*One of the juror-witnesses comes forward to be the SECRETARY.*

Hello.

**SECRETARY:**
Hello.

**JEAN-BAPTISTE:**
I've come to see Mr. McPherson, I have an appointment.

**SECRETARY:**
Yes, I know, but he can't see you until nine o'clock. Would you mind waiting till then, please.

*M. waits.*

*Percussion.*

**CRIER:**
Eight fifty-five.

*Percussion.*

**SECRETARY:**
They're waiting for you.

**JEAN-BAPTISTE:**
Mr. McPherson is not alone?

**SECRETARY:**
No, Mr. Marshall is with him.

*JEAN-BAPTISTE presents himself before McPHERSON and MARSHALL.*

**JEAN-BAPTISTE:**
Good morning Mr. McPherson, good morning Mr. Marshall.

**McPHERSON:**
Good morning.

*MARSHALL shakes his head. Very long silence. We feel MARSHALL and McPHERSON suspicious and M. not knowing where to begin.*

**JEAN-BAPTISTE:**
You know why I am here . . .

**McPHERSON:**
No, but you may tell us.

**JEAN-BAPTISTE:**
Well, to have an explanation of my dismissal.

**MARSHALL:**
As far as I'm concerned, the matter is settled.

*The juror-witnesses who have been "living out" M.'s situations, look distressed.*

**JEAN-BAPTISTE:** *trying to stay calm*
You can at least tell me the reasons.

**MARSHALL:**
Insubordination.

**JEAN-BAPTISTE:**
But I do my work, I follow all instructions!

**1st JUROR:**
I arrive on time, and I don't lounge around.

**2nd JUROR:**
I even try to improve on the work systems.

**McPHERSON:** *sarcastic*
Improve!

**3rd JUROR:**
I get very good results.

**4th JUROR:**
I don't drink.

**5th JUROR:**
I don't hassle the secretaries.

**6th JUROR:**
I tackle more work than the others.

**MARSHALL:**
Insubordination and insolence.

**JEAN-BAPTISTE:**
Insolence! But I've never been insolent, I've always respected my superiors.

*McPHERSON stands up, addresses MARSHALL.*

**McPHERSON:**
I'll be back in a minute.

**JEAN-BAPTISTE:** *trying to restrain him*
But . . .

**MARSHALL:**
Mr. M. there is no point discussing this any further.

**JEAN-BAPTISTE:**
And why are you calling me Mr. M.? Haven't you always called me J.B.?

**MARSHALL:**
That was when you worked for me. Now you are no longer under my command.

**JEAN-BAPTISTE:**
What do you have against me, Mr. Marshall?

**1st JUROR:**
What have I done to you?

**2nd JUROR:**
What didn't I do?

**3rd JUROR:**
What was I supposed to do?

**4th JUROR:**
Become a mute?

**5th JUROR:**
Forget everything, be just a pair of arms and legs?

**MARSHALL:**
I have nothing against you. In fact if we ever meet some day on the street, we might go have a drink together.

**JEAN-BAPTISTE:**
But you don't understand! This isn't just a little inconvenience for me, it's my life, my dream of becoming something that's crumbling.

*McPHERSON comes back in, M. turns to him.*

Mr. McPherson, I've done everything for the progress of the company, and I want to do even more. *He opens his briefcase and takes out a paper.* Look, read this study I wrote, on my own time, at home, on the functioning of the department.

**McPHERSON:** *shoving the paper aside*
Not interested.

**JEAN-BAPTISTE:** *to MARSHALL*
Have you read it?

**MARSHALL:**
That wouldn't change anything.

*Silence.*

JEAN-BAPTISTE: *pointing to the telephone*
Do you mind if I make a call?

McPHERSON:
No, go ahead.

*JEAN-BAPTISTE dials a number.*

JEAN-BAPTISTE:
Mr. Cole Stanway, please.

*One of the juror-witnesses comes to do COLE STANWAY.*

SECRETARY:
Who should I say is calling?

JEAN-BAPTISTE:
Jean-Baptiste M.

SECRETARY: *repeating*
Jean-Baptiste M.?

*COLE STANWAY motions that he is not in.*

I'm sorry, he's not in just now.

JEAN-BAPTISTE:
But it's very important, can you reach him?

SECRETARY:
Reach him?

*Signal from COLE STANWAY.*

No, unfortunately.

JEAN-BAPTISTE:
But you must.

**SECRETARY:**

I'm sorry, it's impossible. *She hangs up, JEAN-BAPTISTE hangs up, slowly.*

**McPHERSON:** *sarcastic*

My boy, no pull is going to get you back into Dutron.

**1st JUROR:**

That's final.

**2nd JUROR:**

It's hopeless.

**3rd JUROR:**

Why fight it?

**4th JUROR:**

Why go on?

*JEAN-BAPTISTE comes back to his suitcase, slowly takes out his rifle. MARSHALL, frightened, approaches M. who, seeing him aims the weapon at him and shoots. Panic reaction from McPHERSON. M. shoots McPHERSON.*

*The JUROR-WITNESSES rejoice, scream like a woman in labour.*

*JEAN-BAPTISTE quickly shuts up his suitcase, picks it up, and rifle in hand, heads for LALONDE's office.*

**THE JUROR-WITNESSES:** *screaming*

More! More! All of them! All of them!

*JEAN-BAPTISTE comes up to LALONDE and shoots him. He goes downstage, puts a bullet in the rifle, and aims it at his temple.*

*The JUROR-WITNESSES are suddenly silent. They then rush to M. and disarm him.*

1st JUROR:
No!

2nd JUROR:
My wife.

3rd JUROR:
My son!

4th JUROR:
I'm not a coward.

5th JUROR:
I have to explain to them.

6th JUROR:
I'm a man, I'm just a man.

*JEAN-BAPTISTE extricates himself and flees.*

*The JUROR-WITNESSES go back to their office work.*

*Music as at the beginning mutedly in background.*

1st JUROR:
I didn't see anything.

2nd JUROR:
I didn't hear anything.

3rd JUROR:
The important thing is to keep on with it.

4th JUROR:
There are no solutions.

5th JUROR:
I didn't see anything.

6th JUROR:
I didn't hear anything.

*Percussion.*

**CRIER:**
Ten twenty.

*A JUROR-WITNESS – CHRISTIANE comes to answer the phone.*

**JEAN-BAPTISTE:**
Hello, Christiane, it's Jean-Baptiste. It's done!

**CHRISTIANE:**
What's done? You got hired back?

**JEAN-BAPTISTE:**
No, I shot my bosses.

**CHRISTIANE:**
What?

**JEAN-BAPTISTE:**
I love you, Christiane, I've always loved you, I'd like to have given you more than I did.

**CHRISTIANE:**
Jean-Baptiste! What are you going to do?

**JEAN-BAPTISTE:**
I'm going to call the police to come and get me.

**CHRISTIANE:**
Where are you? I'm going to meet you.

**JEAN-BAPTISTE:**
No, Christiane . . . I love you. *He hangs up.*

*Percussion.*

**CRIER:**
Ten thirty.

**JEAN-BAPTISTE:**
Hello Dutron . . . I wish to speak to the officer in charge.

**SECRETARY:**
What about?

**JEAN-BAPTISTE:**
It's about the murder that's taken place.

**SECRETARY:**
Can I take the message?

**JEAN-BAPTISTE:**
No! I want to speak to him, it's important.

**OFFICER:**
Hello?

**JEAN-BAPTISTE:**
Is this the police?

**OFFICER:**
Yes.

**JEAN-BAPTISTE:**
I'm the one that killed them.

**OFFICER:**
Where are you?

**JEAN-BAPTISTE:**
In a phone booth at the corner of Park and Laurier.
Come and get me.

**OFFICER:**
Don't move. I'll be right over.

*Percussion.*

**CRIER:**
Eleven o'clock.

**JUDGES:**
Jean-Baptiste M. is arrested and order is restored.

*Percussion.*

*M. is led to centre-stage by the policeman. He is greeted by the JUROR-WITNESSES who surround him, touch him, etc. (c.f. childhood scene.)*

**1st JUROR:**
It's him!

**2nd JUROR:**
It's the killer!

**3rd JUROR:**
He looks normal enough.

**4th JUROR:**
Nowadays you can never tell, it shows less and less.

**5th JUROR:**
Maybe he had a reason.

**6th JUROR:**
Sometime, you wonder . . .

**1st JUROR:**
What's life for anyway?

**2nd JUROR:**
It feels kind of like a camp.

**3rd JUROR:**
A concentration camp.

**4th JUROR:**
Without any guards even.

*The three victims – JUDGES come downstage and form a semi-circle around the group that encloses JEAN-BAPTISTE M. The rifle is in front, towards the audience.*

**5th JUROR:**
Two or three guards for thousands of prisoners.

**1st JUROR:**
And nobody moves.

**2nd JUROR:**
There they are.

**3rd JUROR:**
And on it goes.

*Percussion.*

**JUDGES:**
The Crown vs Jean-Baptiste M.,
For the crime of murder
Upon three counts
For the bereavement
Of three families
Of their means of support
For the willful injury
Of a great enterprise
For disruption
Of the accepted order
On this day of grace
Nineteen hundred and seventy-two.
The proceedings will come to a close.

Let each man be free
To speak what he knows
To speak what he thinks
To do what he must
That justice may triumph.

*Percussion.*

**MARSHALL, judge:**
A verdict must be rendered.

**McPHERSON, judge:**
Society must enforce its laws.

**LALONDE, judge:**
Men must make sure it is respected.

**MARSHALL, judge:**
Society cannot be guilty.

**McPHERSON, judge:**
Because society does not pronounce the verdict.

**LALONDE, judge:**
Men pronounce the verdicts.

**MARSHALL, judge:**
Is Jean-Baptiste M. guilty?

**McPHERSON, judge:**
Of disrupting the public order?

**1st JUROR:**
But there is much more to be said yet.

**2nd JUROR:**
It's more complex than that.

**3rd JUROR:**
We must.

**LALONDE, judge:**
Guilty?

**THE JUROR-WITNESSES:** *one after another*
Guilty.

**LALONDE, judge:**
Is Jean-Baptiste M. guilty?

**MARSHALL, judge:**
Of having willfully injured the enterprise?

*They make a kind of lunge for the rifle, but are stopped by LALONDE's line.*

**LALONDE, judge:**
Guilty?

**THE JUROR-WITNESSES:**
Guilty.

**MARSHALL, judge:**
It's your own judgement.

**McPHERSON, judge:**
We are not responsible for it.

**LALONDE, judge:**
We are simply here to see that the rules of the game are respected.

*The JUROR-WITNESSES begin to circle around M., miming their office work gestures.*

*Music as at the beginning is heard softly in the background.*

**MARSHALL, judge:**
That the game is played according to the laws, according to the traditions.

**JUDGES:**
But we are responsible for nothing.

**MARSHALL, judge:**
It's no use killing us.

**McPHERSON, judge:**
We may be dead, but the rules of the game remain.

**LALONDE, judge:**
And other judiciary bosses.

**MARSHALL, judge:**
As for killing the rules.

**McPHERSON, judge:**
As for killing the game.

**LALONDE, judge:**
As for inventing life . . .

JUDGES:
First of all you'd have to begin to think about it seriously.

MARSHALL:
Until then –

McPHERSON:
Back to work!

*The following lines are taped and mixed with the music. The volume crescendes to its maximum in the theatre, and the lights slowly go down.*

LALONDE:
You must be convinced that you are a link in a great chain.

MARSHALL:
I want your office to be clean.

McPHERSON:
You must love you company as much, if not more than, your wife.

LALONDE:
Answer the phone, be courteous.

MARSHALL:
You spend more time with us than you do with your family.

McPHERSON:
Don't think about what you could do, do what you're told.

LALONDE:
The man that lives according to the laws learns to love them.

MARSHALL:
All together now with us.

JUDGES:
The greatest chemical empire
In the world
Thousands of employees
Dozens of factories
Millions of capital shares
The company
That produces

Kantron nylons
Porlon acrylics
Kraly textiles
Bypar carpeting
Teflon fibre
Coron rop
Lacron polyesters
Refrigerants, Aerosols
Solvents, Peroxides
Paints and Enamels
Dynamite and other Explosives
Frayon
Luco

JUDGES:

Lacite
Dulite
Liners

*The JUROR-WITNESSES begin very weakly and are urged on by the cries of the three JUDGES.*

Louder
Harder
Faster
Louder
All together
Harder
With feeling

*To end with a crescendo.*

Lacron polyesters
Refrigerants, aerosols
Solvents, peroxides
Paints and enamels
Dynamite and other explosives
Frayon
Delux
Lacete
Teflon
Dulite
Liners
Films, tubes, resins
Vinyls, acids, dyes
Insecticides
Cellophanes
Celluloids
Porfal
Dutex
Fibrex
Valar
Cor-flex
Bortel
Nylon

**JUDGES:**

Teflar
Clytar
Katon
Metron
Bucinth
Debrin
Salyn
Diprene
And what have you.
The greatest chemical empire
In the world
Thousands of employees
Dozens of factories
Millions of capital shares!

*BLACKOUT*

## PRODUCTION NOTES

There are several "readings" which can be made of the play. For example:

– Jean Baptiste M.'s colleagues at Dutron act out the play after working hours, to try to understand his actions.
– Actors are staging the play and each might, before the play begins, draw a name to decide who is going to play J.B.M.
– J.B.M. could also be played by a different actor for each scene.
– The play should be staged realistically with a high degree of understanding.

### Percussion

A musical instrument, such as the tympany can be used for the percussion or it can be done on a desk or a metal filing cabinet.

### The Chorus

The readings of the accusation by the Crier as well as the enumeration of the Dutron products, could be done by all the Jurors.

### Beginning of the Second Act

Depending on the "reading" that the director decides upon, the very first scene of the Second Act could be improvised, based on the written dialogue. The actors entering the stage before the trial resumes and learning about an identical story that one of the actors is reading, will in a "theatre game" act out the parts of the characters involved in the news story. By doing so, they can also reveal their personal feeling about Jean-Baptiste M.

### Setting

The name of the characters as well as of the companies could be changed to fit the place where the play is produced.

## TALONBOOKS – PLAYS IN PRINT 1974

*Colours in the Dark* – James Reaney
*The Ecstasy of Rita Joe* – George Ryga
*Captives of the Faceless Drummer* – George Ryga
*Crabdance* – Beverley Simons
*Listen to the Wind* – James Reaney
*Rinse Cycle* – Jackie Crossland & Rudy Lavalle
*Esker Mike & His Wife, Agiluk* – Herschel Hardin
*Sunrise on Sarah* – George Ryga
*Walsh* – Sharon Pollock
*Apple Butter & Other Plays for Children* – James Reaney
*The Factory Lab Anthology* – Connie Brissenden, ed.
*The Trial of Jean-Baptiste M.* – Robert Gurik
*Battering Ram* – David Freeman
*Les Belles Soeurs* – Michel Tremblay
*Hosanna* – Michel Tremblay
*Forever Yours, Marie-Lou* – Michel Tremblay
*Honey* – Jackie Crossland
*Three Plays by Eric Nicol* – Eric Nicol
*API 2967* – Robert Gurik
*Preparing* – Beverley Simons
*You're Gonna Be Alright Jamie Boy* – David Freeman
*The Last of the Order* – Richard Benner